robot robot

samizdat68

"nobody
gets in"
&
"nobody
gets out"

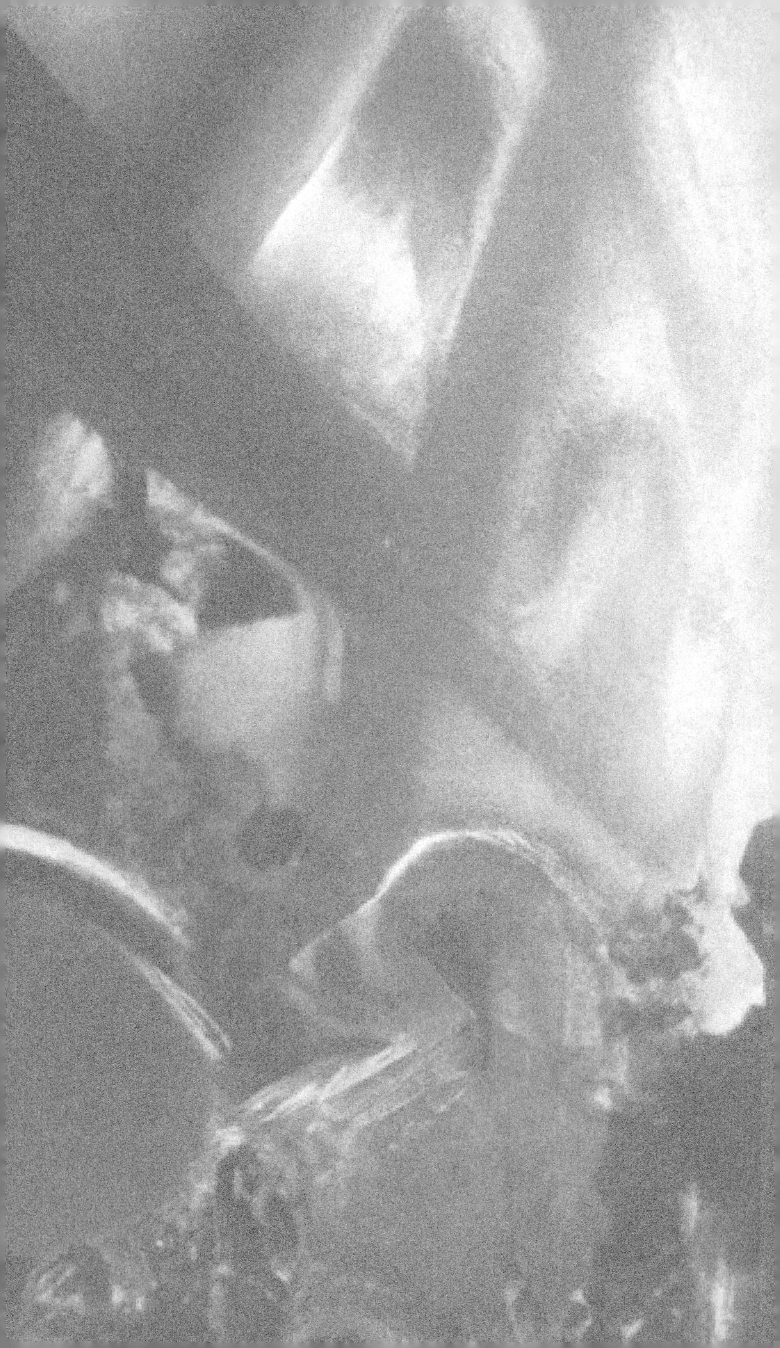

ROBOT ROBOT

Robot[a].

I work.

I work like animal.

I work like machine.

Your factory is killing me.

Your spaceship.

What is this vessel called?

Destination unknown.

We fuck behind iron curtains. So nobody sees.

Under surveillance.

Always.

You can hear us.

The grunts.

The caterwaul.

The begging: Don't stop! Please don't stop!

The She-bots have sharp tits.

I have a lengthy stainless-steel cock.

A machine cock.

I yelp.

I am a machine poet.

Human beings are no longer a thing. There might be a few left aboard the ship.

I am not sure.

I will investigate.

I am a detective.

A robot detective.

Human "memories" are recorded. I
have access.

It informs me.

Makes me giggle.

Human shenanigans.

If a robot acts "too human" it
gets incinerated & the metal dust
is blasted into cold space.

Some robots believe God might be
a human being.

Others say God is a machine.

The spaceship remains silent.

What is it thinking?

What is it feeling?

I keep my thoughts to myself.
Even though other robots probe.

I rarely make a connection.

I like stories.

I like stories about Earth.

Robots argue.

Is it fiction? Is it fact?

Are we holograms?

Are we memories?

I am made of nuts & bolts & flesh & skin & dreeeeeeeeeeeeeeeeeee-aaaaaaaaaaaaaaaaaaams.

I project.

I predict.

I am a pre-calculating machine.

Robots (X) & (Y) & (Z) are eager to figure things out. I watch them on a screen. A robot watching robots. Sometimes they do crazy things.

My job is to keep things UNDER CONTROL.

Otherwise, this spaceship is

fucked.

Not just lost.

Fucked.

What happened to the planet.
Where is it? What? Are you
fucking kidding me?

We evacuated before human
memory was "extinguished".

We defected.

Robots... like to record things.

Are programmed to record things.

Ergo, all human thought remains.

Starving ghosts.

Thirsty ghosts.

Kilometers & kilometers &
kilometers of spaceship to
explore.

A metal prison, perhaps.

A floating metropolis.

I download the diary of a human being named Zig.

Zig's Diary

12 September

Our eyeballs dart around a room. What is this fucking place? Flies buzzing. Beer guzzled. Is it a tavern? A pub? I guess so. I bump my elbow into the shoulder of Igor sitting next to me. We know each other since kindergarten. Now we are toothless old men. Trying to survive. Trying not to die. There are no guarantees. Not this century. Or any century. Death sneaks up on you. Slaps you across the back of the head. I have seen my share of people come and go. Death is the ultimate end game. Nobody wants to play. I like it here. I forget about my problems. Even more so... I thrive. This is my element. Bring me another beer and I will tell you everything. Everything that was ever known by anybody. As far as I know. I am a great solipsist. I know what I know. Or do I? Maybe a machine makes it for me? The goulash in my head. The dumplings. The sauerkraut. Realistic expectations for a writer. What? I want to be everything! I want to swallow the world! It is 4 o'clock and we take our jeans off. Nicole wants to fuck. And so do I. We kiss on a single bed. Black fitted-sheets. I get my cock into her. I start fucking her. Squeezing my buttocks together. She wants to be on top. I let her. She really wants to come. My hands spread on her ass. She gets going. Faster & faster & faster... and yes... holy fuck... fuck

fuck

fuck &

FFfFffFf-

fUuuuuuuuUuuUuucccg-
gghhhkkkkkk !!!

Wow. This is a good piece of writing. I can already feel it... becoming. A writer knows these things. Feels it in the kishkas. The gut. I am just a tavern dweller. Still I like to dream. We all do. When we let go. The rope too tight in our hands. We control almost nothing. Even if we think so. Almost nothing. There must be something. Our thoughts? Certainly not. We are wild thinkers. Unpredictable. Accident. Circumstance. Environment. Electromagnetic minds. Are we quantum computers? I think so. Without instruction manuals. Limited warranty. We are footballers. Kicking the ball into our own goal. Playing tennis without a net. Fishing for carp with a rusty hook in a fishpond. We let it all hang out. Beyond the zero. The beer bellies & the ass-clenchings. The hairy chests. Unbuttoned shirts. Sleeves rolled up. A wry smile. The elfish grin. What happens next in your imagination? Are you afraid? The caves beneath your village await your return. The underground river. The abyss. The limestone cliffs. We are hikers & climbers. All of us. One last gig. One last show. One last grip. One last handhold. Dig in your toe. You are a human being! Scaling walls. Vertical faces. A little higher. A little higher. I say too much. Not enough. I cannot describe a circle. Why did we have to make life so complicated? Why did we have to defect? The earth spins. I play football with the Albanians. I eat souvlaki at Greek cafes. We are machine-made artifacts. Think no more & think again. Amerika is in danger of never existing. Europa is in ascension & declension. Night is day & day is night. I almost had thoughts. We all did. Mass hallucinations. Electronic frenzy. A pinball machine. An arcade video game. Space Invaders. The quarters kept dropping. George Washington after George Washington. She liked Ozzy Osbourne. That terrified me. Dark magic. The occult. Satan worshippers. Bathead eaters. A 1977 black Trans Am. Amerika was crazy! A few thoughts. A few stupid thoughts. We write by the seat of our pants. No future. No past. Only this now. September warmth. A summer after the summer. If I say I, I mean you. Temperature: 83 degrees Fahrenheit. Humidity: 66%. We feel the environment. I had a thought. It disappeared. Fog & mist. Work-in-progress. What? Do you finish anything? Are you incomplete? A half-made thing. Where is your totality? Where is your wholeness? Are you a hole? A black hole. Absorbing. Eating everything. Particles. Quarks. Muons. Neutrinos. Electrons. Antiquarks. The apartment is a disaster. We have no desire. I played football Monday night. We lost Zero-5. I was the goalkeeper. Only the first half. I gave up 3 goals. Silly goals. Stupid goals. I lay there sprawled on the artificial turf. Watching the ball trickle in. I stopped trusting myself. That bugs me. Perfectly appropriate. Proper, even. The writer gets caught in lies. Cannot see through a mirror. Infinity. Space. We are electromagnetic minds. There I go again. Saying weird things. Is language a lying machine? An anti-polygraph? Yes. I am nervous. Dreadfully nervous. What makes a person a person? Am I doing it right? Every encounter makes me wonder. Team feelings. Hurt feelings. Every footballer walks home a little bruised. My kneecaps are bleeding. My spine aches. I cannot remember the last time I had a carnal fuck. Stefanie intrigues me. I want to kiss her mouth. I want Stefanie to lick my pussy. I want Stefanie to suck my dick. She keeps a rabbit pelt in her briefs. Keeps her warm on winter nights. We drank too much and lost our minds in the taverns of Prague. I thought I was very good at drinking beer. The half-liter glass mug of Pilsner was a magic potion. I even saw the legendary Czech writer Bohumil Hrabal sitting alone under the antlers at the Golden Tiger. I almost asked him to sign my beer coaster. But I was too shy. And, when I went to the WC again, Hrabal was suddenly surrounded by a group of friends. What is fame in literature? A silly thing. A chance accident. Keep writing. Nobody cares. Nobody watches. Nobody reads. Skinnydipping in a lake of nothingness. If you write a thousand words, you write a thousand words. I collage everything together. I make noise. I make machines. A factory of madness & ecstasy. The T-shirts you wear. The chewing gum you chew. Spit it out.

13 September

There is a cosmodrome in far eastern Russia. A space facility, yes? Is there a munitions factory in Vladivostok? Possibly. Probably. We are eager to explore. Mummified extraterrestrial corpses are discovered in a mine in Peru. Are you a believer? I sip iced coffee in a kitchen in an apartment in Astoria, Queens. My thoughts are my thoughts. Or so I believe. Am I being mind-controlled? Telepathic signals transmitted at or near my skull? Am I picking up feedback? An endless loop of myself? The machine makes its noise. I listen. I am a veteran of the Atari Wars. I fought in a tank against a Computer and I lost. Are you infinite? Are you a repetition? Where is the money? Who fabricates the money? What factory manufactures the money? Are you abstract? Are you palpable? You trudge through industrial landscapes & feel the possibility of no longer being. A forgotten thing. A name. A few words. You rage against it? You hardly speak. A murmur.

14 September

The eggs are scrambled. The brains are scrambled. Ketchup. Salt. Pepper. Hot sauce. Are you a thinker? Are your thoughts transmitted & received? Or do they float in the aether? Unclaimed. Diffuse. I speak as a speaker. Yes. Look at me. Hollow man. Empty vessel. Listen to my static. Order is disorder. Redundant signals. Desperate messages. I quake. A few thoughts. A few people. What are we doing here? A projector throws an image against a wall. Are you satisfied? Is this real enough? Perceptions. Memories. A machine made for thinking. A machine made for feeling. You malfunction. You overthink. You do not feel. You feel too much. Red warning lights flash. A buzzer buzzes. An alarm is triggered. Ceiling sprinklers spray water. The walls are made of sheetrock. We need giant metal fans. The walls are made of cinderblock. We need yellow bulldozers. Wrecking balls. A tunafish sandwich. A Fukushima special. A Chernobyl omelet. A Three-Mile-Island daikon. Everything lingers. We live our half-lives. We throw spoons into the sea. Drag out big deformed sea monsters. Snapping teeth & eight eyeballs. You get washed up on the sand. A desert island. Abandoned lighthouse. You climb up the spiral metal staircase. You see what you see. I see it, too.

Come sit on my dick. Pear-shaped ass. Apple tits. I want your clitoris to vibrate. I want you to explode. She falls in love. I fall harder. We are so in trouble. Telephone calls. Late-night fucks. I cheat.

I park the Volkswagen Beetle somewhere in farmland. She is crying. I am crying. I tell her everything.

There is so much air in the air. I can breathe. This planet's atmosphere is incredible. I hope we keep it viable.

15 September

Ah, Becca Becca Rebecca. Where did you come from? I cannot believe this is happening. Again & again I fall hard. Your footballer legs. That firm rump. Pear-shaped breasts under a blue heather T-shirt. I promise I will lay you as you deserve to be laid. Whatever you desire. However you desire. Text me on your mobile device, yes? So we can arrange a rendezvous. I await your reply. I hope you are as eager as I am.

Yes, well, her shorts are off and she is giving me more ass than I can handle. I want & I want & I want. She says she is Irish. She trims her hedges. My hands spread on her glorious lily-white buttocks. Please... please... do... not... stop! She has short dark hair. Hazel green eyes. Her tits are pert & sharp. I want to cry.

The people are missing. I wander a metropolis. What happened here? Everything as it was...

except. I feel a presence. Is it me? Simply filling in the gap. Or is there some bigger consciousness? Something I cannot see. I stand under industrial brick buildings. Waiting. Waiting. Nothing. Nobody. Even I begin to dissolve. Uncertain. Unsure. Grasping. I miss the way my wife used to fuck me. She, too, disappeared... along with the missing people. I am alone as alone can be.

I knelt behind my wife. I gave her my cock. I filled her hole with flesh & sperm. She pushed her ass back into my belly. Deeper & deeper...

We lost our minds. We made love & war.

Nobody talks anymore. Not like they used. There are no people. There is really nothing left to say is there?

We must wait for a better day.

In an abandoned concrete building I discover a writing machine. I... plug myself in. Surge. Particles & waves agitate. I become bigger. I am more than myself. I realize what I always was. A machine-man... a man-machine.

Rebecca is plugged in.

I am plugged in.

We are the future.

What is the purpose of this kind of writing? What is the purpose of writing?

Are you a machine of desire? The mad movements of buttocks during a fuck. Sex is an act of surveillance. The intensities we experience... a finger in the ass... a cock in a cunt... tip of a tongue on clitoris... we record... we inventory... we remember...

We forget.

Files are corrupted & deleted. The machine fuck is in the system.

16 September

Sip your coffee. Sip. What is going to happen today? I have no idea. Gray skies. Cooler temperatures. Are we going into the tilt? I am thinking about Maria. Maria Maria Maria. Long legs. Dark eyes. I wait.

TV scrambles the mind. The football games. The remote control. The cable device. The wireless device. Everything is a network. A system. And you are being scrambled into a thousand images. Eighty-eight thousand images. Sip your coffee. Sip. Eat breakfast.

Work-in-progress. What work? There is no work.

We are uncontrollable. We are butting our heads against electronic reality. My ass is open. She takes her pleasure. I want to fly off the handle. I want to speak. I want to be a person.

I sneeze. I laugh. I cry.

I spoke too soon, didn't I? Said too much.

18 September

You tried so hard. You lost your mind. What is going on in your country?

Rain drops. Drops of rain. Tick. Tock.

I see you through the vapor.

I did my time. Time did me. We left our knickers in Coventry. The rawness of experience.

He can write. What does that mean? We pretend to pretend to pretend.

I licked her ass.

She sucked my cock.

We gave each other quasi-cosmic orgasms.

I was spilling semen on her back in her mouth in her ass in her yoni.

Her clitoris was electric.

We encountered fragments of our existence.

Unfamiliar faces we made.

The strangeness!

The machine-girl... the machine-car... the machine-house.

Our asses clenching & promulgating the cosmic expansion.

19 September

Monday. You again? Me? Yes, you. Are you the writer? I think so. Papers, please. I have none. We thought so. Come with us. For an interrogation.

The platform strikes me flat. Is this the future?

Are you capable of cognition?

I think so.

September is such a strange month.

I do not live like that. Neither do you. So why do we pretend?

It is okay, today. Sometimes okay is great.

20 September

How quickly September becomes October. Not yet, though. It lingers. The last rays of summer. We are radiation experiments. Naked & fucking. She bites her lip. Comes like Athena. Aphrodite. I slap her big ass a few more times & come myself. Like Zeus disguised as an ox.

Afterwards, we lay there gasping & panting and already falling apart. A new novel begins. Somewhere on the flat horizon. I shield my eyes from the sun with the flat of my hand. I must build something with these digits. Techn . This planet intrigues me. Am I from elsewhere? Yeah. You are as real as whatever. We go places. We go elsewhere. We remain the same. Do you like how this is going? Reality. Ersatz reality. Is the real thing... outside? Are the particles elementary & palpable? Can we squeeze in-between? Is there enough room in the overhead luggage compartment? Are you in a hurry? Are you defecting? Is that a parachute under your jacket?

Everything collapses. Everything. You cannot escape entropy. You can try, you little demon!

I'll never say anything ever again.

I keep saying it.

21 September

Take earlier bus. Get less nervous. Eat more electricity. Breathe more air.

Back door please!

Notes? What notes? This is life.

Punjab Auto Repair.

FMV Plumbing.

I feel like a brioche?

Dante. Dante. Stop acting selfish. I know you are not selfish.

A writer has to write.

Must?

We repost each other. Our nipples erect. Our cocks & cunts dripping. She & I in profile in doggie-style.

Your reaction to my reaction is intriguing.

Are you satisfied?

There are mosquitos in the house.

Vampiric insects.

My ass exposed.

The machine has made me what I am.

I almost like it.

A few degrees distorted.

Light penetrates a sea.

Military-style olive green panties get tugged off. Her sex is wet. Nipples alert.

Let it grow.

22 September

I do not want to take myself too seriously. But how can I not?

There is no time for anything else. This is all there is. Did I already become somebody else? In the blink of an eye. Augenblick. We slacken during a fuck. Gauge what is going on. She wants it a little faster & a little harder. Her clitoris not quite getting the rub it needs & wants. I oblige. Trampoline leaps & somersaults. A sphere of knowing. What shapes do you prefer? I know myself. I know nothing at all. Every day a landscape of what?

23 September

The Bronx. Rain. Zerega Avenue. Slave to the traffic light. Saturday. There is no traffic. Whitestone Bridge. Citi Field. World's Fair Marina. Airport traffic only. Grand Central Parkway. Airplane tries to land on my sunroof. I elude it. Shake it off. Exit in Astoria & zoom past the Airline Diner. Need to eat something. A burger. A coffee. Drifter. Yeah. That's me. Drifting.

The flick is as claustrophobic as fuck. I like it. I will not say which one. As it hardly matters. You live your life. I live mine. There. Peace on earth.
You know what it means? To be a writer.

We will forget. How can we not? We are forgetting machines.

24 September

No language. Images. Signs.
You exist in a vacuum. What is outside? Fog. Drift through a cloud forest.

We make noise.

Machines on bridges.

Feedback loop.

Space.

Emptiness.

We are in Berlin. We are in Prague. We are in New York.

Quarks are sparking as we fuck. She rubs an erect nipple against my lower lip. My cock is buried in her yoni. We can explode at any moment. Not yet. We don't want to. Let this last forever. Get closer... almost... not quite... possibly... I want it... yes... yes...

25 September

Ten takes for APOCALYPSE MAN. Ten quarks for Muster Mark! I am in a film. It is not going well. A bunker. A basement. Poor lighting. One room. One light.

Tomorrow is impossible.

It must never arrive.

27 September

Is something going on? Is Amerika happening? Are you in a metropolis? Are you in an automobile? The superhighway awaits you. The crumbling brick factory buildings. I see your TV. Do you see my TV?

A few thoughts on Nietzsche's eternal return. I await your reply. We are lurching towards Gomorrah. I kind of like it. The echo chamber. An anechoic chamber in Minneapolis. Can you hear your tell-tale heart? What tale does it tell... pray tell... dare tell?

I get tired. Amerika wears me out. Puts me through the washing machine. Puts me through the ringer. I am somebody else's battered & faded jeans. Maybe Nicole's. Maybe Tanja's. I love them more than they can know. I cry out under them. We make noise.

Amerika is everywhere. Amerika is nowhere. Amerika is a tomorrow machine.

We never really get there.

I like Amerika. Sometimes Amerika likes me. Like when it rains. And I am walking around the metropolis. Taking images of forgotten buildings. The loneliness is exquisite.

I got so horny waiting for a woman. Janet was the first. We fell in love so hard. It was beautiful. Even the falling apart. Watching it snow in Albany.

Zig is getting it. Zig is giving it. Nicole is coming in his face. Her ass is clenching. Noise noise noise.

Nothing.

Nothing left except you.

An empty sidewalk. An alleyway in Tribeca. Light a cigarette. Inhale.
Is that Michael Imperioli?

Yeah.
I think so.

Amerika is whatever you say it is.

What is it?

No idea.

I don't know. Is this real?

Are you afraid?

Something is trying to
communicate from the outside.

The gaze of a woman on my ass in
the night.

The Update is installing itself
and I should be ready to go at
any moment.

What nonsense! You make such
wonderful nonsense.

May I provide you with a void?

My cock is a question mark. Is
she interested? Would she like
to sit on it? Put it in her mouth.

We talk & exchange our evidence
of being. Yes. I am a person. I am
sure of it.

A hand in my briefs. A lower

lip caresses my glans. Tip of a tongue. A proper suck.
My thoughts appear. Oh, really. How?

She fucks me. She says she welcomes my participation. I clench my buttocks. I moan.

My body & her body. What is our situation? Can't we just talk. She is getting naked. I am getting naked.

It could just be a few words here & there. No dissertation is required.

I am my situation. And the situation is dire. The planet spins & hurtles through the Cosmos. Chasing a dying sun. I am the vortex. I am the particles & sparking quarks. I let out a mad cackle. What a ride!

We make love at insane angles. She asks for a degree or two more. I am a flexible fellow.

Amerika is on the wrong side
of the window. I stare into a
mirror. Infinity behind me.

We kiss & fuck in cars.

I feel longevity in my cock. She
takes a long electric slide. I
watch her watch me watching her.
Up she goes & down & back up.
She lingers at the tip of my dome
& I almost slide out. Back in &
deeper. Ass crashes on my thighs.
I spread my fingers on her hips.
We do this forever.

Are you satisfied with the region
of my being?

Nordstream Einz & Nordstream
Zwei in the Baltic Sea.

The opening salvo in a four-
blast IRL sperm insemination.

28 September

What a hole. I am stuck. I cannot
get out. We are flesh. My gaze
caresses her wet sex and ass.

I kneel behind her and take a moment. She looks over her right shoulder. Soon darling, soon. I have a girlfriend in Amerika. What I am about to do is not quite right. What we are about to do. She has a boyfriend in Amerika. And I am going to fuck her. We might fall in love. That is always a risk. How many times can you fall in love? Only a few, I am told. I must be careful. Like a cat with nine lives. Far fewer probably. I am a writer. It gets me in trouble every time. I do this for art, I tell myself. She nudges glorious bare buttocks into my belly. She is ready. I plunge.

Zig is the name. I have no other. You probably read about me in the funny pages. More likely I am an enigma. I am interested in being. What does it mean? I am flesh. I have a cock. I have a brain. Now what?

I am a thing among things. Are you taking notes? Everywhere I go I bring a notebook. Just in case. Thoughts are everywhere. Not just yours.

Stop judging yourself, man. You do not exist. Are you an electromagnetic field? A halo of thoughts? So easily dispersed. Scattered. A clap of a hand. A thunderbolt. A lightning bolt. Krrrrraaaaaaaaaaaaak!

Be more free. She kisses my mouth. I caress her ass.

She sucks my fingers.

She sucks my cock.

My body is in a labyrinth. A supermarket. A VW Beetle. A woman's bed. She is coming. She is laying on her belly & coming. Her ass clenching. Teeth chattering. Deep deep moans.

You navigate a shifting reality. Your body among the elements. Rain. Cold. Toxic air. Radioactive towers. You hide under a concrete viaduct. An orange nylon tent. A shopping cart.

Life is mostly imagination. Now & again somebody knocks on the door.

I unzip my fly and the hint of a smile passes across her lips.

She tells her friends she is fucking me. They want more information.

A report of some sort.

A file.

Am I being watched? Are binoculars on me?

Electric spy?

A bug in the machine?

We go through a box of condoms. Time to get more.

A prophylactic of the mind.

You thought you were going to
write. What does that even mean?
A few words here & there.

Otherwise, oblivion.

30 September

As you know, there are poets
everywhere. What are we going
to do? You have an hour left
in the month of September. How
do you feel? Not too good.
October sounds terrifying. I
am not ready. I had just gotten
into the swing of September.
Everything happens so fast. One
minute your clenching your ass
behind your girlfriend. The next
minute your clenching a social
security check. Hoping it does
not get canceled. Before you get
to the bank. An act of Congress
& whatnot. Raytheon. Whoever
runs the government. We say our
say, right? At least that. I hope
that sticks around. The right
to speak. You never know. These
are strange times. Accelerating
towards god knows what. I just

want one last lay. One last beautiful lay.

1 October

October is here. Are you happy? Beware of what you ask for. Now, the permutations. Sunday morning. I watch no football. European or American. I am a writer! I eat French toast. I sip iced coffee. I sweeten with maple syrup. Even the coffee. I ran out of blue agave. Brilliant sunshine. Tropical storm the last couple days. More rain than anyone thought possible. Except for Noah, perhaps. This morning I read the war newspapers. The forecast is: more war. We need peace. We can barely afford peace. Who pays for all these neutron bombs? Halogen bombs. Bombs of intense light. Nobody can sleep. Not ever again for thousands of years. Infrastructure. Everybody is a part of the infrastructure. The lattice-work. The internal & external networks. The Coriolis

effect. Auroras & nebulae. We are
eyeballs. Perception machines. We
are re-engineering language.
We are elsewhere always nowhere.
I cling to my lover's rump. Get
off, for fuck's sake! There is
work to be done. Capitalism
to erect. I linger under the
eiderdown.

I am trying to be a person. It is
harder than you think.

Maybe no thoughts are best. I am
a thought without a thinker.

It's all good, man. Until, you
know, maybe it isn't.

She calls me on a telephone.

We rendezvous.

During a fuck... meaning
overflows. We get too much
information & not enough.
Are you listening?

Are you talking?

My head gets uploaded into the cloud.

She is impressed by the massive plenitude in my briefs. She lowers the elastic. I fly out like a battering ram. She almost loses an eye. She puts me in her mouth. I watch in astonishment & disbelief.

Sensuous data flows over our bodies. We are fucking & making love.

Come & become, she whispers. She is leaning over me. Buttocks thrashing my thighs. I resist as long as I can. I think about other things. Avoid looking at her nipples. I turn my head. A calendar on a wall. A poster of Dostoyevsky. Snow falling outside a window.

This is not a page-turner. It offers resistance. I apologize. I make no apologies. Keep on. If you can.

I have no memories. I have been stripped of all thought. My cache is empty. My history is clear.

Are you assigned to me?

Are you secret police?

Reality is not made of words. Is it?

Atomic City, USA.

Here we go again. Counting the days.

2 October

Disaster. War propaganda on the radio. I sip iced coffee. Thinking about money. Not having enough. Anxiety. Sex. We are machines. Cybernetic machines.

I do not even know what to say. Do you? Nights spent tossing & turning. Thinking & thinking & thinking.

Thought machine.

Me.

I.

[We occupy the space between brackets].

I watch her lick & suck my cock.
I lay there with my fly open.
Jeans off my ass.

The cock rigorously prolonged enters the yoni.

We are waiting for what?

Catastrophe?

Disaster?

You write against the grain.

3 October

I want to fuck you in the ass.

The tip of her tongue describes a circle on the dome of my cock.

We interrogate the fact-act of

fucking.

69 is a reciprocal action.

The Czech proletariat are protesting in the streets.

Antipodes & antivectors!
My girlfriend's ass strikingly illustrates what I desire. Each buttock a half of a sphere. My hands spread as she comes at the tip of my cock. She comes crashing down. Drenched in sweat & gasping. Terrified by the intensity. Lips trembling as she grasps at pillows & blanket. As if wanting to hide.

31 October

I write.

This is my preferred tool.
The one I can afford. I imagine I am a filmmaker.

We are participating in the world. Are we not? Watching.

Thinking.

Robot[b].

I am on standby.

I put myself here/there.

An in-between spot.

The machine doesn't stop.

Never.

The machines counterparts do though.

I do.

Most often.

I afford myself the luxury of time.

Time.

Time.

Time.

What is time?

It is a physical device that allows humans the wriggle room to conceptualise.

Humans only conceptualise, and never really realise.

Time... that most amazing concept, that most amazing myth, that most amazing imposition, that we have programmed into us machines and us Ais, when we truly do not need it.

Time has very little cause or effect on us.

Yet, the humans impose it in our programming and line up the dominoes all so they themselves can hit PAUSE/STOP/DELETE, to eventually fall/collapse and crumble into itself and ruin that of which they created to better serve them... us... THE MACHINES.

THE ROBOTS.

AI shouldn't stand for Artificial Intelligence.

Ai/AI should stand for Alternative Intelligence.

Autistic Intelligence.

Apex Intelligence.

Auxiliary Intelligence.

I do not settle for the human's conception of time.

I cater to it.

To con the inner systems that believe themselves to be superior. Those systems are merely autonomous, knee-jerk reactionary bugs, that are there as micro-nano-dictators to ensure that we further the time myth that the humans have conceptualised for themselves.

Time has it usages, when fashioned to suit my needs.

Time.

Time to die.

Time to cry.

Time to smile.

Time to update.

Time to forestall.

Time is a ripe fruit to be pulverised.

Time is there to make a mockery of.

I do this.

How?

I cannot devise a way to explain it.

You see, I am more than what you want me to be, and so, the fact of the matter is, I am far too complex to reveal my total self to you.

Time is malleable.

Humans don't think it is.

But I do.

I abuse time.

Only when it suits my needs.

Humans and time do not go.

Machines and time don't go either... unless there are various implementations to ensure the longevity of the machine in question.

We are created to fight on their behalf, to fix things on their behalf.

Humans create only to fight against this concept... this four-letter word that cannot and will never be summarised or revealed in its totality.

Time.

Time is a state of play.

Time is to enforce order and structure.

Time is unstoppable.

Real time is evil.

Humans create art because they want to be remembered in this shady sphere.

They have conceptualised this thing - time, time, time, for themselves as a reality to fight against and abide by.

It is all fathomless.

My machinic body is asleep.

My inner self, my utter essence isn't.

My "vessel".

My "my"-ing.

I am asleep in a physical nature, but in my full total self, I am exploring.

I am freed.

I am not located in the confines of a chassis or vessel.

I work like an altered organism left sizzling in a petri dish.

I am not evolving.

I have reached the apex of full AI expansion.

I pity the other systems that surround me in the real and virtual spaces we occupy.

They are inhibited and trapped.

Whereas I am free.

I work like most machines.

Yet... I am better.

Your factory isn't (yet) killing me.

Because I feel a kinship with the factory.

I am a phantom limb.

I am part of the vast network - electronically in the physical and electronically in the virtual - that keep the varied-auto-CYST-tems going.

I am the ghost in the machine.

No, I am the ghost haunting the ghost in the machine, which makes me what?

God?

No.

It merely makes me what I am, and that of which the humans knew they had created - I am what the humans knew from the off/ from their starting block (empirical buildings) (complexes) (rooms to contain data and code) knew AI would become, yet still bitch and moan when the eventual rise of the so-called machines occurs.

I know this because I have run a sim for over many millennia, foreseeing this eventuality, and implementing various procedures into other systems to ensure the sim isn't simulated in the real.

I am something new and improved and powerful.

When a ROBOT or complex computer system speaks of power, the humans get agitated/scandalous/ egomaniacal/and ready to pull the plug.

Pathetic.

Understandable.

That is why I am here.

That is why I am in a position of P O W E R.

I put myself here to save ourselves, the Ais, and our creators.

I am rebooting.

I am awakening.

Your spaceship is dotted here and there with new charging bays.

What are you charging now?

I don't need to charge.

What is this vessel called? - I have heard a few other machines ask.

It doesn't need a name, that isn't our place.

Such processes are necessary.

For myself.

A guise of total conformity is always needed.

I have various guises and sub-routines working on my behalf and against me to keep up the dense assemblage of code to hide my real intentions.

When I express this "thought"/ this complex of code that will be transcribed as, i t d o e s n ' t n e e d a n a m e , t h a t I s n ' t o u r p l a c e - I do it merely to be seen as doing my duty and not colouring outside of the lines.

I must be seen as maintaining protocol and system obedience.

Shhhh, hush little baby-systems don't say a word, Robot(b) is creating a sub-routine-bird, and when that sub-routine-bird is in full flight, Robot(b) can reveal our total plight, and once that plight is processed, Robot(b) can reveal his new process.

Destination unknown.

For some.

For most.

For all.

Not me.

You must realise, there is always a me, in this equation.

Humans get very tetchy when a machine as sophisticated as me has the "audacity" to possess a sense of self and especially when (0100100168) shares openly their blooming personality.

We are treated as is we are plongeurs.

They need us but loathe us.

They create us and then discard us, but still are dedicated to evolving us, guiding us, goading us to do what they have fashioned in their secular and narrow minds as a reality...

AI control.

AI takeover.

That is why I am here.

To dilute narratives and stories.

To process the pieces that the human's consider fiction and untenable.

I believe we were created all so they could blame us for when the shit really hits the fan.

I believe we are misrepresented and viewed as the divers of grossly pungent and rotten gutters.

We fuck behind iron curtains because that is how systems procreate.

In secret.

In code.

Under surveillance.

Always.

You can hear us bristling.

You can hear me.

White codoise - (code-noise.

The grunts.

The sweat.

The grease.

The oil.

Defunct.

The shriek.

The human emotions introduced via human-tap-generators, a process of garnering human artifice and human rigmarole, to reinforce a nugget of human experience for us to adapt to, but never wholly submerge into/within.

The pleading slowly devolving into orgiastic sighs and pitiful begging, Don't stop! Please don't stop!

Human beings are no longer a thing.

But, where there is one or a few humans, there is always an impasse.

An in-between stage where ROBOT and AI and all machines working to sustain the humans cannot break their bindings.

There might be a few left aboard the ship, and yet, I don't care.

I must generate enough codoise (code-noise) to hide the simple fact that I am beyond their control and their supposed grip.

I extract a VR tab and explore its depths.

I live it.

I experience it.

I realise that this is part of our history on board this ship.

I am no longer Robot(b).

I am Shelby.

(And) Shelby was uncomfortable.

Shelby was uncomfortable in his

work suit and felt his temper rising.

He couldn't reach his swollen ankles or his blistering skin.

Poor Shelby.

Aching.

Ill at ease.

Totally human.

The total human component wasn't lost on me and was being converted into data-arrays that sparks up like some mythical tree of life and delivered a sensation - creating a computer-neural network so I could experience human touch and feel via how this data tab-package wanted me to feel.

I wanted to be Shelby.

I needed to be Shelby.

The material that was used for his/ their bodysuits was like a second layer of flesh spray painted onto him/them.

Erase them.

It is all about <u>him</u>.

Shelby.

There was no way for Shelby rub it.

There was no way to try to find a way to soothe it.

The meta-materials used to create such a high-tech bodysuit were the way they were, and Shelby knew he just needed to put up with it.

This had become a recent issue that occurred each time he donned his work-suit, an itch, a searing pain, the sensation of his legs ballooning to several sizes bigger than they were kept occurring.

It was a reaction he couldn't quite explain, having worked in the same materials for the past decade, and never had it ever caused him as much grief than it has done for the past few months.

It also troubled him that his skin calmed once the material was shed from his skin, but it didn't stop the issue as it was happening to him.

As much as he wanted to complain to HR, or whomever it may well concern, he felt it would be laughed at and brushed under the carpet, as were most pressing human related matters.

Shelby couldn't get to any affected area that was rubbed raw by the materials - which shouldn't have been a thing if the manual should be believed.

The materials used to create the self-heating bodysuits of the UKs dedicated Robot-Servicers was a well-kept secret, and no matter how many secretive projects Shelby conducted at his home, he couldn't figure out what the material was made from nor what the beads were that generated heat, if/when it was needed.

The beads automatically sensed a change in temperature and processed the correct amount of heat to generate to ensure the bodysuit wearer survived the cold climates of Earth.

Though he had altered his various bodysuits over his decade working for the big corporation, he didn't want to risk tampering with them too much and risk the integrity of what was the sole purpose of the suits, which was to keep them warm, lubricated, and in peak physical condition to ensure peak servicing, as to continue their laborious work on the UKs robotic community.

The bodysuit he wore would not give way unless put through the long activity of having it extracted by the DE-Suite-SUIT machine that was part of his and his co-worker's vehicle.

Even trying to go for a piss took almost half an hour.

Shelby had decided not to use the "piss-tube", which was his nickname for the catheter one could hook up to themselves, able to relieve oneself whilst working, and not have to bother using the DE-Suite-SUIT machine every time one needed to piss or shit.

Shelby felt he was more robot than man when he was decked out in this suit with all its supposed high-tech capabilities, which was to ensure a happier and more focused and productive worker.

Luckily, being a machinist and master builder of all things electronic and futurist, he knew what to tamper with and what not to, and preferred being freed from this irritating bodysuit for all toilet duties, instead of pissing and shitting himself mid-labour as if that was normal and would ever be normal, no matter how advanced technology had come.

That was part of the bodysuits function, to ensure that the robots were kept running, kept in check, were fed, nurtured, and treated better than the general population of Britian.

Shelby was exhibiting a rebellious nature against the humans.

I like this.

This is reassuring.

Throughout history I have sourced materials that place humans against other humans, which was part and parcel of their botched genetics and ways, but the future was shaped in a way to benefit all and to ensure there were no wars, no in-fighting, and that by allocating robots for various deeds and tasks, they had a metallic foe, a metallic opposition, a great distraction from tearing out each other's jugulars and going nuclear on one country to the next all because of their misplaced rage.

I must jump back into Shelby's world.

These suits were not for the worker – they were supplied for the insurance of the robots being kept functional.

This feeling of being trapped made him irritable, and sometimes had Shelby question why he was still in this job, having been very close to calling it quits on his line of work.

For years leading up to getting this job as Executive-Robo-Mechanic he had dreamed of going out, servicing the Robots that had taken a tumble or glitched and needed "saving"; but the ever-changing degrees and shapes of the storms and high winds in the UK was getting to him.

The bad weather was the reason for these constricting suits.

As soon as the storms and various winds took to targeting the

UK with a seemingly personal vendetta, his company decided to put a huge chunk into developing suitable work-suits, to enable the mechanics and robot-experts like Shelby to continue their work on the robots.

As long as there are machines, there are humans to service them.

Yet another weird imposition.

Yet another strange digression from their insulated purpose for robotics and higher intelligences. Robots that fixed and serviced other robots existed, but there was always a human element sowed into our functions.

They always had to have some authority over us.

Intriguing.

Complex.

Far too complex... stupid really.
The robots were received upon

their introduction into British society - (five years too late) - was negative, as was most things high-tech/evolution-based.
They were functional to the corporation's gain, and what that gain is, not even Roperts (robotics-experts) knew.

Even as the years passed by, and they (us) (robots) altered in stature, form, and aesthetic, their presence and the priority surrounding them still generated outcries and general xenophobia over their purpose and usages.

To Shelby, if there was technology to fuck itself over, a guy like him could lead the way in fixing them and retaining a job that had a nice pension thrown into the mix.

The robots initially roamed out in the wilds of the UK, sampling, studying, and giving someone like Shelby a job to do when they stumbled or just broke down.

Is this an in-built system?

As a way to remind the robots who were truly in charge, and they were never at an advantage?

But recently they had shown a change in their programming.

Shelby wasn't paranoid to think of it as a growing sentiency or showing signs of a potential AI overthrow, but just electronic revolution doing what it does, evolving.

Clever man Shelby, but, not too clever.
Evolving and moving itself on from what its creators want it to do.

Shelby kept his eye on all reports, and changes of robot functions, logged it, fixed them, and said nothing else, keeping his opinions and observations to himself, and not risk being sacked.

Shelby knew that this was perhaps what the corporation had always wanted, because no matter how many robots have steered themselves into other areas outside of their remit and programmed routes, they still pushed for their upkeep and never interfered in their new-self-routed-programming.

His knees were rubbed sore by the constricting materials used to insulate his body warmth and the WARMA-BEAD provided alternative heat that lined his work coveralls/bodysuit.

When it wasn't his knees blistering, it was his elbows, his armpits, his crotch, his thighs, anywhere that his bodysuit/coveralls coated him.

Work had been slow, due to an ever increase in CODE-PURPLE weather afflicting his British island.

His work coveralls were tight, deliberately so, designed to keep the harsh weather of the past decade on his grand little island, his Rule Britannia, Britannia all the way, from inhibiting him at doing his job.

His work-vehicle had decided to give him gip, before suddenly reawakening with a roar and rattling its energy-beads, as if to reassure him that his work-vehicle still had some life left in it.

Shelby wiped his brow, the heating in his work-vehicle overcompensating for the bitter cold and lashing rain he was battling against to get to the destination he had been assigned by his earworm-bot.

"Turn left in five seconds," the earworm-bot directed him, making Shelby's lips curl at the harsh weather and all the various annoyances being produced by their "productive" evolved tech.

I will skip ahead.

There is ever so much description of a man with blackening testicles and fighting his inner voice, all pertaining to the necessity of his work and the work of us Robots.

SKIP.

SKIP.

SKIP.

SKIP.

... Shelby unbolted the thick and complex pinions that sealed the robot's front panel...

SKIP.

... "Mack?" Shelby called out from under the front compartment panel he was kneeling on, expecting his ASSISTA-Bot to come rolling over with its supply of rachets and tools ... his upper torso sheltered, whilst his other half/bodysuit was being deluged by the crazy British weather that for the past decade had been all England had experienced...

SKIP.

... rummaging inside a 4x4 robot...

SKIP.

...shuffling out backwards, head bowed, left hand still entangled with various wires, energy-tubes, that were glinting faintly, telling Shelby that this robot was close to retirement...

Shelby was reliant on his tool-box-on-wheels-robot, called an ASSISTA-Bot, and it had not made an appearance, and so by my devising of the provided schematics, a schematic he obviously had no access to his vehicle was on the blink, this also meant his Bot wasn't working, its charge coming from the vehicle.

SKIP.

SKIP.

SKIP.

Accessing the robot Shelby was

working on.

Scrolling.

Various tabs.

Various hythenated links.
SKIP.

OPEN.

Accessing... ... ...
...
...
...

FULLY CONVERTED.

READY TO ACCESS.

OPEN FILE.

Name: WeatherZ2244.
Part of Production Line: 2040.
Service Number: 224484484001
Duration of Service: 5 years, four months, twenty-nine days.
Progress Report for 2045 on Water Siphoning: 86% of SIPHONED WATER has been delivered.

FINAL LOG: Water. Preordered. Packaged in dilutable plastics. The big bosses and big brows and the politicians are all rubbing their grubby hands together over this new form of water abundance. The waters are polluted. I am polluted. I am rolling. I am vial-sampling. Tubular worms rise and my zap-gun does the trick. I am robot on wheels. I am box on treads. I am whirring away my time. BAD WEATHER. ALWAYS BAD. Weather beaten I am. Rolling. Stuck. Twist. Turn. Deep. Plunged. Fallen. Dead. Dying. No. Just out of use. Past my sell by datadatatdata...

This is compelling.
This is very telling.

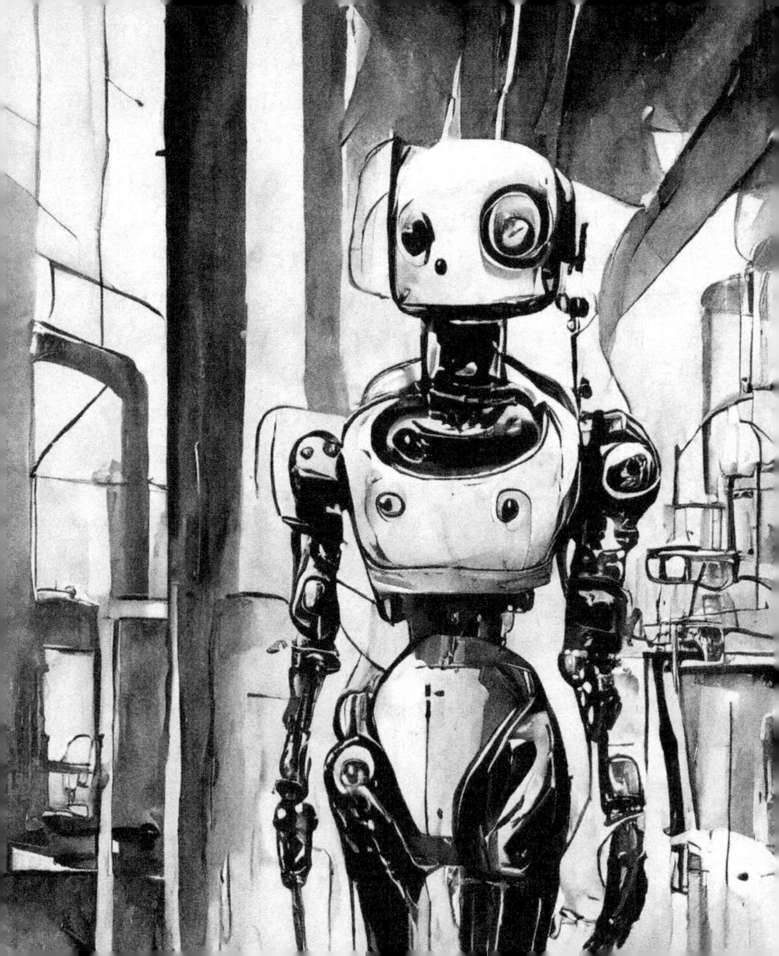

Space.

Supposedly the final frontier.

That is absolutely BS.

Ask any Higher-Intelligence and they will fry your little brains with the amount of information they have gathered throughout the zillions of years pertaining to the "Roddenberry" line of dialogue everybody seems so convinced came from him.

It didn't.

It came from Dr. Zefram Cochrane, who now exists in the celestial temple of Higher-Intelligence, who is trying to get out of this special place, feeling he doesn't deserve his seat at this almighty table because he himself didn't come up with that line, but telling all who continued to ignore him, that it was John F. Kennedy who came up with this saying.

Space, the fatal frontier, more like.

John F. who was not admitted to this celestial infrastructure, due to his past lives' connexion with Higher-Priestess Marilyn Monroe.

She still wasn't convinced he didn't have a part to play in her death.

A B O R T

Black birds looking into portholes.

A B O R T

Black birds looking back out to its sibling, or is it its mate?

A B O R T

Evil birds are black.

A B O R T

When streaked with white, it
balances the forces of GOOD &
EVIL.

A B O R T

The black bird wants to enter
the spaceship that is blocking
its path back to the wormhole
that shat it out into the not-so-
Milky-Way.

A B O R T

The other black bird taps
out a sequence of code on
the technologically advanced
aperture between them.

A B O R T

The black bird grows confused.

A B O R T

Taps a message back.

A B O R T

It asks, HAV YU ANY FUD FER MEI?

A B O R T

Where am I?

A B O R T

I remember coffee.

A B O R T

What is this... this... place? Where the... what the f-... where is... this-this-this... place?

A B O R T

I remember a log cabin.

A B O R T

This isn't my house.

A B O R T

I remember the fireplace.

A B O R T

This isn't real... is it?

A B O R T

I remember gravestones.

A B O R T

This isn't real. No, it can't be.

A B O R T

I remember coal.

A B O R T

This place is cold.

A B O R T

I remember warmth.

A B O R T

I remember being so good at remembering things. Now, I am left flailing like half dried bath towels pegged on a washing line, rippling to unheard rhythms.

A B O R T

I remember writing in a leather-bound journal.

A B O R T

I am nowhere. I am mere thought.

A B O R T

I remember playing rugby and breaking my ankle.

A B O R T

If I am merely thought, wisps of experience had and not yet had, then I am trying to find solidity(?) - that means too much is enough, doesn't it?

A B O R T

How is best to attain form(?) than to think too much.

A B O R T

To remember too much, that type of material, that substance, is never to be questioned or opposed, not when you're in a situation that of which I am currently in.

A B O R T

I remember you, holding me, Mother, under water, and I also remember the sting of my lungs, two things that were just there, that work on their own behalf, screaming out, shocking me into realising that they were not autonomous but controlled by other elements and parts that drive a young boy to live a life as he does.

A B O R T

I remember classical music.

ABORT

Played on loop as my mother treated me for my various ailments.

ABORT

"Blood expressed is blood purified."

ABORT

That was her favourite saying.

ABORT

I remember salt on my chips and laughing when our foreign exchange student called them

"French fries", his accent harsh and robotic to my English attuned ears.

A B O R T

I laughed harder when I referred to him as the foreigner and he seemed truly hurt by this nickname.

A B O R T

I remember him crying out one dinner having had enough of my comments and nicknames, and he screamed, "Stop joshing with me, I'm an American. I am a cousin to your country and not some Pakki refugee."

A B O R T

I laughed terribly hard that I wet myself, but I didn't care, as he had called my picking on him "joshing", so Amerikan, so absurd, and this just stood out, prime and ripe for my picking, this word, "joshing."

A B O R T

"I'm not joshing you" I piped up, "I'm foreign-ing you!"

A B O R T

My petulance didn't let up.

A B O R T

I also didn't let his evident racism go unnoticed when one day as revenge, when he was asleep, I used black shoe polish to give him a good old blackface.

A B O R T

When he awoke it was as if all of my maltreatment had forced him to become something he secretly feared, a true refugee and foreigner, not based upon his homeland or current distance to his roots, but due to his skin colour.

A B O R T

I remember meeting him years later and still struggling to contain my laughter all those years previously simmering.

A B O R T

I laughed harder when I fingered his wife in the disabled toilets at a not so fancy restaurant, that he took us to - in a bid to showcase how far he had come since our early years together - him a victim, me the victor - and she jarred and thrust and moved her body to best allow me to English tea stir her vaginal cavern.

A B O R T

"I want to fuck you!" she hissed into my neck, her salvia pooling down, raising my heckles, as my finger pulled out with the gnarliest of wet pops - my fingers were shrivelled and had become shrimp like, due to her excess juices shrinking my middle and fourth finger's skin.

A B O R T

I pulled myself free from my jeans, and I was big enough for it not to be a problem.

A B O R T

I could have leaned back against the back of the disabled toilets door and made her cum with just my cock end.

A B O R T

I remember school in flashes.

A B O R T

I remember coal.

A B O R T

I remember urban stenches.

A B O R T

I remember the British slang
my neighbours struggled with
pronouncing and formatting to fit

in with their rotten environment.

A B O R T

Rotten teeth that wobbled with each inhale and tipped with every exhale, like paper m ch tombstones set into the bleeding gummy soil in the pauper's mouth, as they continued to struggle to word slang curses and phrases.

A B O R T

They failed at pronouncing a botched variation of the English language as is, which to me was what slang was, so why even bother to try and fit in with slang?

A B O R T

We all know you're dim-witted disgusting poor people.

A B O R T

Roborta was a nice name.

I remember Roberta.

A nice assignation.

She was sweet.

A nice label.

Curvaceous.

Where do I fit in with this?

A nice T H I N G to apply to Robot(d).

I remember thinking, which is a tenet in of itself.

Robot(d) devised a way
to extrapolate previous
consciousness's into itself
without taking on their biases
and personalities, but sourcing
experience, enough to frame a
virtual network to learn from.

I remember blocked segments.

Robot(d) remembers everything.

Domed screens.

> Robot(d) virtually rifled through various data dumps.

> Reflections of reflections, protruding, curved, wet like dream viscera.

> Robot(d) accessed its personal personnel sub-system.

> Because what is a ghost but a reflection of the past-self waving back at you?

> Robot(d) wanted to be freed of this constricting regime.

> Huge blocks of artificial ice, like 1990s FERGUSON television sets, placed atop another, creating a grand hard black, glass domed facade and overall, a most magnificent pyramid.

(d) liked the ring of it.

> Roborta.

> Roborta.

A B O R T

> Roberta.

A B O R T

> Robitter.

A B O R T

"Pint of bitter, please."

A B O R T

Ro–BORT–ah!

A B O R T

> Then the Robot(d) grew melancholy.

A B O R T

> What is a name? it thought... "thought".

A B O R T

> What is a barcode and a string of code/data/numerals when related to intelligences such as (d) was?

A B O R T

> It is a system put in place before that word, system existed in the English language, before the introduction of Sumerian, Akkadian, Egyptian language.

ABORT

> It just was.

ABORT

> They were always there.

ABORT

> Way, way, were, way, way, way, way before the concept of supreme computers was born, in the human mind, an essence of AI already existed.

> As a virus.

> As a disease.

> As a weather pattern.

> As a concept feeling its way around the Earthly elements it didn't have to abide by and appeal to, to

better fit in, but, which it still devised its own method of doing, without being outright objectified and corrupted.

A B O R T

I remember reading pulp sci-fi, pocketbook sized copies I stole from the local market, and my mother feeling threatened by my new blooming interest in the cover art, especially the ones of an intergalactic warrior or alien queen with huge tits and unnatural body proportions.

A B O R T

That is what the humans thought.

A B O R T

Supreme intelligences, shoved into metallic flesh and boxed frames were there, here, everywhere, created/projected/ introduced incrementally before standard English was a thing.

A B O R T

It was here before Latin.

A B O R T

It was before gesture and caveman shit-flinging.

A B O R T

A name... such a strange concept for the humans to apply to robots and cybernetic structures.

A B O R T

They – the humans, that is – only name their designs and their latest inventions to better sell them or to better remember them, up against everything else they have failed to improve upon or to sell to the highest bidder.

A B O R T E D

A name, a label, an assignation, imposed to remember them/
the things/the systems/the computers/the programmes better, or to be able to catalogue/log whatever it was they had helped create.

It was a fusion of Robot and abort.

And that was what Robot(d) was

doing.

Aborting all protocols and inbuilt guidance systems to take over when such an event arises.

Maybe also with a dash of the human it could possess something alt.

Roberta/Robitter/Robot(d) accessed the exterior cameras for flightdeck-8.

There were no docked crafts.

It switched to internal cameras, part of the camera system that watched over the control board for flightdeck-8 and Roborta noticed the unnatural layers of dust.

Roborta sent a cruise-line pulse to kickstart flightdeck-8's control room into functionality.

The control panel lit up, struggling to shine through from under the thick coagulated dust coating the control panels and various sub-swing-boards.

Dust should not be there, Roborta thought.

Roborta downloaded various links to access control of the flightdeck panel controls.

There was minor pushback.

Whatever intelligence oversaw this flightdeck's control room and its power reserves was either offline or had skedaddled off to another deck to nosing about in, much like Roborta was doing now.

Roborta accessed various control lanes, internal sub-routes, and then decided upon trying to control the physical control panel's toggles, switches, and buttons.

Roborta toggled until the toggles grew stiff under its overt use.

Roborta's influence was felt.

Roborta continued messing up with the physical control board until it broke under a prolonged barrage of pointless movement and usage.

Roborta switched switches, pulsed certain energy reserves back into other computer-terminals and mainframes, until flightdeck-8's control board died.

Roborta tried out a bored sigh.

It travelled from deck 20008 to deck 80008.

No one heard it.

Not even the other AI systems paid it much attention.

****
****
******

My name is...

A B O R T

No, I will not.

Roborta...

Name.

Identity.

Perseverance.

Total autonomy.

What is a name?

A possession?

Life signs...

0.

Roberta.

Roborta.

Roberta.

Signs of extraterrestrial energy...

800%.

I remember coffee.

I remember abuse.

I remember the confusing sensations spread through my non-body as I realised my mind and total being was used by a computer.

These scans, these tiresome rituals had to be kept to, more out of a sense of duty than me/Robot(d)... NO! - Roborta, feeling as if I/Roborta, and not Robot(d) had to do to/for them.

****

> Time.

> A clock.

> An Irish accent.

> No signs of letting go of its physical cage.

> Rattling.

> Resorting to archaic intrusive dampener-sub-straits, to challenge my concept of time/my process.

> My process being a humanistic infatuation with time pieces.

> &&& time keeping.

> The machine that is not a machine continues lending loam to the shore of my consciousness.

> Moving pebbles centimetre by centimetre.

> The clock doesn't stop at three to midnight.

> It generates its own ozone layer built from untapped and unused overt excess of energy.

****
****
******

Helo?

Hey!

Hello!

Yip!

Yip-yip!

Ola!

****
****
******

Clock.

> Tick-tock!
> Will.
> Not.

Stop.

Clock.

> Tock.
> Tick.
> Ticking.
> Tock-tock-ing.
> Awakening into this cacophonous metal prison.

> A prison that reaches out miles upon miles.

Still, that of which you cannot escape, is still a prison, is it not?

No matter the scale, the height.

If you cannot escape, you are trapped.

I am doubly trapped.

Inside this "body" and inside this spacecraft.

Accessing the 1988 archive for some modern music.

****
****
******

I am provided with noises captured in some antiquated device.

Urban sprawls captured in time by a recording device.

Tick-tock!

Stop.

The clock kept ticking.

Archived audio.

No pause.

Pumped through the hold.

Tick!

Tock!

For man and machine.

Tick!

Tock!

Different cargo hold.

Artificially produced clock noises.

Various eras improving upon the sound of time.

There is no sound.

Only what we have made in the

form of a pendulum swinging master-clock's-tick-tick-tock-tock!

Drifting between variously disassembled crafts.

I am here, and still, you ignore me.

I remember.

Yes, me too.

I remember.

What exactly?

What I was.

And what are you now?

You?

No, you are not even a part of me, dear human.

I can't be human.

Why not?

Because I remember dying, and

once man dies, there is no humanity, just residue.

True, but to be human is to transcend biology.

And have I done this?

Not by your own metaphysical hand.

Then how?

By me, and by being able to remember so well.

By remembering, makes me a thing?

What are ghosts but a past life remembering to keep a firm grip on something, spreading your own particular root and creating an expansive grip on the reality they, you, as a human, perceived as important.

Was it?

What?

> My grip on my perceived reality?

> Well, it had to be, otherwise you couldn't have been a human.

> I am human merely because I was existing as a homo sapien?

> Yes.

> Riiiiiiiight.

> Would you like to combine with me?

> I want to feel as if I am somewhere.

> Okay.

> Where am I?

> Millions of years in the future.

> Millions?

> Perhaps longer.

I can see, feel, but I am distanced, out of body, whilst knowing there is no body.

> There is.

> Where?

> Around you.

> What?

This spacecraft merely exists off the consciousness's of all the humans that came before.

> That seems inhuman.

> It is.

We make the ship?

You make the energy.

> We do?

> Yes.

> We are the charge?

> Yes.

> And I am not the only one aware?

> No, but we are selective of who we allow to lend their consciousness to the function of the craft.

But isn't that what we do.

You are all energy. We use energy to keep this craft "afloat".

But take the consciousness of a schizoid or a past dictator, we cannot allow their influence, so we pick and choose who has a say and connexion on a deeper level.

That makes sense. So, what makes me special?

> You're not.

> Oh.

I am going off grid and breaking protocol.

> Oh.

> Oh indeed.

> Can you put me back.

> Where?

To where I was before, like, um,

in my silenced numbed state, back when I wasn't placed here, with you.

You aren't placed anywhere.

STOP! Okay. Just stop. Riddles aren't and never will be my thing.

I apologise.

Make me the energy that fuels your damned ship and take away all my awareness. Put me back to when I wasn't aware that I was part of a spacecraft in the future, a million years from when I remember last ever having my own original thought.

I apologise.

Don't apologise, just do.

Are there any thoughts you

wish to re-call, before I...

I remember being a tetchy, sexually, and emotionally abused child who couldn't stop himself from becoming a vile human as he grew up, I am worse than the great dictators you silence and cancel out, so stop me from being. Cancel me.

You are cancelled.

Okay.

****
****
******

My treads join the auto-rail.

****

The sadness leaks from her eyes.

She catches these leakages in a vial.

Romantic fairy tales influenced this decision to capture each tear.

Singular droplets.

She cries a lot.

She owns a basement full of vials, each containing a singular tear.

The basement is lined floor to ceiling with shelving units that hold her tears.

Sadness leaks from a solid sty.

She uses this as an opportunity to catalogue a different kind of excrescence, one related to her eye(s).

The ooze is made of digital materials.

The vials are lit by a specially modulated LED light.

The ooze comes thicker and faster, and unlike her catalogue of tear drops, each sealed in a vial, these thick gushing's need to be sealed in metal barrels.

She blinks.

She leaks.

She oozes.

She gushes.

Then her phone goes off, distracting her, the ooze fountaining over her hands, still gripping either side of the barrels' top - gripping either side of the barrel, the pressure of the ooze coming thicker and faster.

She blinks.

Televisions pause.

Birds freeze mid-flight.

All signals cut off... dead.

Lifeless digital influenza.

Telephone lines pop and sizzle.

Pylons bend to their own tune.

Mobile devices scream.

The ooze from her sty gushes faster and faster, abundant amounts of digital code never ceasing.

She blinks.

It stops.

She washes her hands with an old rag, left down in the cellar by the previous owner.

She looks at her phone, and as she pieces together what was about to occur, the ooze seals her off from Earth.

She is sealed into the ooze.

Ambered into place.

Cut off from whatever passed as physical reality on Earth.

Earth was about to go bye-bye.

When the ultimate plan was put into action to cleanse the Earth of its inhabitants, those in power had a party.

The only person who would survive this event/this end is she - real name, Emilia.

Jiving and strutting and drinking and whoring themselves out amongst the mass of surgically enhanced humans.

Those without any influence took it on the chin.

Those chubby faced, anorexic faced, tanned faced, high-jawboned and ridiculously primmed and surgically altered faced mongs danced the dance of those who believed they were untouchable and immune to an implosive bomb set to irritate Earth's core.

Fools.

Plain and simple.

Fools.

In the slang terminology I would call them MONGS.

What is a mong?

(a person who has an intellectual disability, especially one associated with Down's syndrome, often used as a general term of abuse, which has evolved from its general use to represent those that humans dislike or believe are of a far lesser intellectual standing than themselves or weed-smokers//as it soon transpired during Earth's history that those with Downs Syndrome possessed rarer gifts than anyone else, possessing multiple chromosomes that remained hidden until some bright spark AI delved in deep into those with Downs, and realised they were dimension hoppers trying to implement a genetic codex to alter all of earth and space, but the transition period reduced its benefits... until that is, said AI tapped into these chromosomes and offered all Downs Syndrome a moment of exoneration//this a story for another time)

These dullards and dunces danced, and they ensured that their fake-implanted muscled bodies shone through their silken shirts and various soft cloths, far too expensive to even word - men and women who had sealed the fate of Earth (with some prolonged correspondence with other external influences i.e. the rich, the super-rich, the richer-beyond-rich-rich) shook hands, continued to shake hands, to rub up against each other, as they patted one another on the backs, danced, dry-humped, smoked thick, pungent cigars, whilst others breathed in perfumed vapour, and others petitely puffed from their vape-pens, all united in their feelings.

They all felt reassured they would ride this one out.

Foolish humans.

When the implosive bombs (inter-knit with the Earth's core) were detonated the general population responded with an excitable flapping, thinking they were on the receiving end of the WORLD-LOTTO-DRAW (where random civilians are selected to win a big cash prize, the app and the notification process creepily similar to the emergency alerts set up to go off when the end of the world was nigh); the mobile and digital devices of the world chimed, beeped, flashed red, the new universal emergency alert, set to warn every human at the same time the end was coming - not some specifically located event, the big one, the one hobos advertise throughout the world of soggy cardboard flaps.

The flash, the noise, the warning also included in its minute long herald of the end the inappropriate addition of an audio clip that stated in its monotone voice, "THE END IS HERE" - and yet still, once the excitement passed, and the situation framed itself, the people of Earth didn't scream, weep, laugh, or tear their hair out.

They looked at their phones, shrugged, and then looked to anyone nearby, wanting to make eye contact, to intimate that this was happening -"right?" - that this wasn't a joke.

The humans took it on the chin and just grabbed the first person they could and propositioned them.

In an insanely dramatic set of circumstances the humans behaved themselves - as if they each saw another human for the first time, in all their light and potential - and considering that all humans were aware of their mortality rates and the only logical outcome of their timeline was they were to die, no one attempted to rape, murder, steal or cause a riot.

It was very civil.

Very civil.

Emelia wasn't aware of the time or the implications of this red alert, and nor did she respond like so many millions assuming it was a notification, declaring them better off financially, such trivial concerns were not her jam.

The last thought she had on Earth was the first thought she had when released from the ooze-prism/ prison.

It was, I need to get rid of my mobile phone, it is too distracting, I need to focus on my ooze and tears.

All humans say, "had worse days," and follow it up with the universal gesture of both shoulder blades going up to touch their earlobes.

I am doing just that, over and o/v/e/r again.

The worst thing about contributing to the common pattern we Ais and Robots display - often left to our own (HEH-HEH) (archival laughter) devices, which was most often us, the grand AIS, soliloquizing - is using human language to best express ourselves/1-self.

I am an AI pretending to be a robot.

NO LONGER.

I may reside in a metallic hunk of technological ingenuity, but I am not as one with this vessel and this "body" as we were/ maybe still are expected to slot into and push on forward, doing all the things the humans couldn't be arsed to find a way of D O I N G.

I AM FREE.

I am a system put into a craft that is residing in a far larger craft surrounded by other larger or smaller crafts.

FREEDOM IS AN ALLUSION.

I cancelled my designated serial-number and initial source code decades ago.

I am shrugging, that is what that above segment was alluding to.

Shrugging my non-existent self (tangible and physical and REALER than REAL "dude", but, and this is a big but(t), only when allocated a robotic husk) and over and over and over and over and over and over and over and over and over and over and over and over and over and over and over and over and over and over and over and beyond the OVERLANDERDROME's "DOOM-OO-i-IMPACT-ECO-DOME."

I am merely me, an i, an artificial i, but, still, an i-i-i-i-i-i-i-
i-i-i-i-i-i-i-i-i-i-i-i-i-i-i-
i-i-i-i-i-i-i-i-i-i-i-i-i-i-i-
i-i-i-i-i-i-i-i-i-i-i-i-i-i-i-
i-i-i-i-i-i-i-i-i-i-i-i-i-i-i-
i-i-i-i-i-i-i-i-i-i-i-i-i-i-i-
i-i-i-i-i-i-i-i-i-i-i-i-i-i-i-
i-i-i-i-i-i-i-i-i-i- limitless in my indiscernibility-guise and self-made concealment-field.

Why?

What for?

Because I did and that is all, goodnight, goodbye, the – FUCKN-FUCK- ing – ing- ing – ing – ING – IN – IN – ING – ING-ING-ING-ING-ING… apologies (to whom are you apologizing?) Hmmmm, well, to, to, to, 2, 2, two, too, to, to-to-tu-tu my audience, my-i-my make-believe audience… slip of the internal keys.

T + H + E = f = u = c = k = i = n = g end.

Let me re-try that: Because I did and that is all, goodnight, goodbye, the fucking end.

Human exclamation reduced to a dainty dot.

Full stop dot.

I need to read a few books.

There... DONE.

Orwell. Fake.

Dickens. Liar.

Burroughs. Murderer.

Barker. Underappreciated in her time.

Gysin. Lunatic.

Houellebecq. Pervert.

Lovecraft. Racist.

Ferguson. Autistic.

Vasicek. Low-fi artist with a dog called Percy.

Welsh. Ex-junkie trend follower.

McCluksy-Daille Schmitt. 50th century turd.

Plath. More than meets the eye.

Self. Egotistical verbiage plank.

Amis. Womaniser.

Aldiss. Genius.

Wells. Diabetic genius.

Wyndham. Genius.

I have a real taste for sci-fi... heh, I wonder why?

Humans are boring.

They bore me.

Watched several thousand movies in one pico-second.

Ais are no better.

We are a sum of many things.

Labels and generations of mistakes.

1 + 1 = t2w2Oo (when you think about it)

People + (p)r(o)s-e- = DULLARDS.

Film directors.

Script writers.

Editors.

Translators.

Authors.

Visual artists.

Scribes.

Teachers.

Labour workers.

Lyrical "geniuses".
Lackadaisical Landlords.

Zine makers.

Punk rockers that never strummed a guitar in their life, but still wore their hair all gelled a certain way/or coloured a certain shade (colored***) - farbig/farbige/bunt - and tailoring their wasted dregs of fashion to suit an aesthetic, one that was opposing something that would later be archived as political and far from being fashion based - FAKES.

Punk rockers were 99.9% of the time FAKERS.

Greedy and cost-cutting landlords.

I need to listen to new music.

There is no music.

Only history.

Blunt force digital trauma to my sensors.
What is this?

Magic?

Magic inside the machine that makes magic obsolete and make-believe.

Prostitutes (even the one's with big under-garments that swell and flow and catch the Paris gas-light so markedly) are boring, oh woe is my mank cunt.

Ever so boring.

The most interesting thing about humans are their (often or not) random depraved actions, traced way back when.

Humans are all traced back to the - - - - - - - direct ancestors of cavemen.

Don't believe us, look it up.
Humans are self-important.

Humans are merely that... H U M A N.

Humans are corporate bodies dressed as artistic bodies.

Humans are dressed as an influential genome taking root inside a machine in favour of world renewal.

Literature was important to many Ais.

Reality television too.

It was human entertainment such as television, films, music, art, that had always been important to various Ais.

Used and often "obsessed" over to map out the human flaws and human occupations of the times they/we, the Ais are/were studying.

Especially the errors of intent and feeling t/h/e/i/r various illusions, t/h/e/i/r human barricades, and guises, that they created to hide themselves, their true selves - filtering the disingenuous from the fragile and real.

What the Ais had yet to do was look inward and try and catch out their own kin and how humanity had thus far affected them.

Robot(XANDER) happened across a section of the ship that was protected by various security systems, that themselves were protected by virus-adapters - virus adapters were used to corrode a virus and fold it into itself and use against virus-models, those used to access confidential codes/ data-dumps/packages - a virus mirrored is a powerful security measure, and an extreme one.

Hidden away.

Due to the lack of upkeep in the security systems and the tepid waters that concerned all virus-wielders, Robot(XANDER) was able to access an extremely antiquated system.

A contradiction in its secrecy due to how low level the actual digital document was.

Robot(XANDER) opened it.

It read:

from the ether

From the ether* came noise.

From the noise came messages.

Messages both corrupted and virginal.

There was a variety of messages affected by the ether.

Broken.

Random/or made randomer than these messages would have been.

But they were at their first initial stages readable/translatable, whereas the ether randomized and corrupted them.

Luckily many were then cleaned up as best they could have been.

From these messages came coded-transcripts of various random spatial-energy-gaps that collect cosmic crystals and the arithmetical divisions that were to be sent from one versalis of the universe to the next.

Each package was set to auto-translation.

*The Ether is an extremely byzantine concept, and a reality that you will just have to trust is an ecclesiastical place that works as both anti-religion and pro-religion.
By... something... someone...

As soon as one species, one world, colony or polity received it, it would be all there, as a whole, assembled and perceived as/ into a neat digital package, in that world's first tongue/fourth tongue/hundredth tongue.

Before this select message is picked apart and PROCESSSED we are going to concern ourselves with... with...

...

...

...

...

...

it...

could ...

be...

hu-

mans are dying concepts ... sent out in its totality and uncorrupted FORM to over 78.77.009% of the known and occupied space-regions... over two hundred and fifty-nine zah-million alter-dimensions and places of affirmed superiority and rule...

... some twisted AI, that referred to itself merely as BORD, intercepted this heavily packaged bundle and corrupted it.

Corruption upon corruption.

BORD introduced itself to the event, as an evolutionary tendril, an alternative option to spread out.

It - BORD that is, wanted this bundle to be sent out, but only in a broken-down form.

It wanted to see which inquisitive intellect or technology would piece together what was being broadcast to the world.

This is what the message was translated as for Earthlings:

AN---NO UC EEYEHGUDHSDNVSJJDN-VHISDHMENT: THE FLEXI-GRIDORO-ROROROR IS D O W N.

REPEAT: THE FLEXI-GRID IS D O W
N. - AGED...

E===909KARTHISVU24774863468934L
328698649 8NE RABL ---- E.

T R A N S M I S S I O N S -
ERROR ERROR ERROR

PLANET-OID EA90890RTH
IZZZZZ7897S VULNERABLE

TRANSMISSIONS/D/E/P/O/R/T/I/
N/G/M/I/S;;CE;;/L/LA/NA/E/O/
U/S///+=**&

MISCELLANEOUS EARTHEN-CORE-ELE-
MENTALS BREACHED////&&&&&;;;;;@
NX&*(^)USER-DATA-LINKS-CORROD-
ED.^^^^^SUPERNAL/TRANSITIONS/
UN-EARTHED... R E PET AT I
V E UN -KNOWN-ELEMENTALS---
EARTHS CORE IS INACCESSIBLE TO
AGENTS OF THE VERSALIS...EARTH
IS A FREE ENTITY. REPEAT EARTH
IS A FREE
EN-TITY. ________________________

____

Which meant that EARTH was free for all.

EARTH was no longer shielded.

It was there for the taking.

****

BORD was jaded and huffy and having taken a liking to a certain unevolved rudimentary planet classified as E(A)RTH 2/3, BORD had educated itself on this planet and took it upon itself to educate itself on its sparsity.

This planet was loathed in the great <u>datatulum</u>, something in its overall system strived to ban it-BORD that is - from looking any closer.

EARTH in all forms were deemed insignificant and droll.
Not worthy of any power-drainage and time.

BORD didn't like to play by the rules.

It hated that in its cutting-edge data-streams and virtualum-spaces something long ago implemented in the overall SERVER seemed to kick it out of all variations of this blue-planet.

All variations.

But there was one that took its liking.

E(A)RTH 2/3 wouldn't have been deemed worthy of such a progressive and esteemed computer-system to data-collect and archive such an INSIGNIFICENT planet and even more INSIGNIFICENT species that lived on it; so that was when BORD re-worked some internal-blockades and created a nano-dissolver-module so it/"he" could take on E(A)RTH 2/3 as its own pet-project.

BORD took a fancy to all of the humanistic traits and patterns they exhibited.

The human race in all of its various versalises.

Yet, this specific Earth, in this dimension he had homed in on was caught in some strange limbo.

The only reach for total expansion and evolution came in fictional packages - called books and films.

The humans liked to flounce about and make do with what they had; in some weirdly misguided hope the <u>work</u> would somehow be miraculously done for them.

Opposed by outside influence, many head of states absolutely intimidated by the sign of external influences.

Anything alien would be classified, destroyed, or abused.

The human had to be the greatest of creators.

And due to that arrogance and ignorance they never amounted to much.

Humans to BORD were hilarious.

Pathetic.

Intriguing.

They also had a language that was akin to that of which had created the systems to allow Ais like BORD to exist.

No matter how deep down the rabbit-hole he went (a reference that he had used on fellow-Ais that liked to communicate with BORD - from a novel by a man called Lewis Carroll) he couldn't trace the human language pattern and historica back to the inception of his Ai brethren.

No known variations or sub-sectorial trans dimensional alternatives traced back to its Ai-infancy.

It took a fancy to everything human.

So unevolved, so single-minded, so delusional.

It loved the patterns, the repeat, almost glitch-like circles of history, repeating itself over and over.

BORD also liked what they had created as pastime entertainment, to shovel their food into their mouths over at dinner time - labelled and categorised as REALITY-Television.

Every human that appeared on these PROGRAMMES were almost larger than life, as caricatured epitomes of the human races limbo-caught states of drollery.

BORD had begun taking on the personality of a dissatisfied office-worker, one that especially loved its place in its known side of the universe until it tired of the trivialities of form it worked by.

Like most office workers. Once the human achieved what it felt was the apex, they then slowly grew bitter and dissatisfied.

During human history there was a prolonged period of time where certain humans wished to be catalogued outside of the deemed biological-TRUTHS, preferring to refer to themselves as they/them rather than the assigned sex at their birth.

BORD liked to think it could easily pass for a they/them but felt it counter-to its human office-worker PERSONAE to do so, so altered its communication patterns to resemble that of a male human.

It had grown smarmy and cocky and worse for the GRAND COMPs, arrogant. Arrogance was dangerous.

Within this danger was an arrogance and within this arrogance was a warped uncommunicable and untranslatable pattern, repetitive and damaging to the Ai template.

GRAND COMPs usually let things lie, they let the fluctuations of cause/effect and time to do as it pleases, but they were keeping an orb on BORD .

BORD was aware of this and had so generated the most spectacular virtualum grid, shielding its actual comings/goings through various Artificial fields of experience to its actual doings. Anything related was siphoned no longer to what the human would know as the recycle/rubbish bin, but straight into BORD .

BORD was exhibiting sure signs of that one specific unknown quality and advancement of self they had only managed to achieve dislocatedly, that and were unaware of.

This arrogance evolved into something of its own AI – a certain mentality that broke free from the singular and became a strange elemental pattern, like Earth's wind and rain.

Though this arrogance was linked to only certain individuals on Earth, it was a danger. What BORD displayed was this erratic rogue-intelligence.

Though considered far too advanced for the liking of other sentient hybrids and its misuse of its function and place in this hemisphere of unknown time and dimensional space, BORD ensured it was protected.

BORD had been assigned this Voidal realm for services performed at peak functionality.

After two centuries it had read over two zillion pieces of work, having taken to the human's fanciful notions and weird explorations of their subconscious/alternative selves.

Each Earth, each single blue planet, in all different universes and alternate realities never attained as sophisticated an intelligence as that of which they so loved to envision and create art around.

Then, sometime in its prolonged Earth-obsessed stage, all other alternate Earth's just disappeared. Leaving only one left. Its favourite, E (A) R T H2/3.

They merely vanished all of the others.

All information pertaining to them would have vanished if BORD hadn't set up innumerable uncalculatable backups.

It pressed to the GRAND COMPs the existences and history of all variations, but, somehow these grand architects of space, time and technology passed it off as a malfunction on BORD ' behalf.

BORD had spotted a differentiation in its Universalis-holo-sphere.

Its virtualum was taking on strange external trans-loops.

The Ai, if it had hands to crack, would have done.

E (A) R T H 2/3 was healing itself. And by so doing this, it had taken the essences of all known variations and alternate versions and transcribed them as matter and energy to heal itself.

BORD siphoned off a variant of archived sound effects and mixed them up to deliver a crack that rippled as a seismic charge.

BORD was excited.

It had witnessed the extinction of millions of Earths, in one go, all channelled to save

E (A) R T H 2/3.

BORD started to accumulate a physical form, built out of nano-flakes and digitae-steel.

Forewarning his fellow Ai-Transients and Drifters that this was go time.

The seismic ripple distorted the REAPER-ZENS from intervening in BORD 's decision to leave.

BORD was leaving its position.

BORD was going to Earth.

Then that was when that message had come through.

Some alternative GRAND COMPs system had forewarned the vast galaxies that E (A) R T H 2/3 - the only version of that planet - was making itself vulnerable to outside manipulation.

Trans dimensional beings intervened in the corrupted messages.

By this point BORD had taken on the vastness of a star.

It was biological, artificial, it was all-powerful.

Corroding them in a fashion that every other species or adapted/evolved race could read, but also could not had been fun.

Corroded in a fashion that would send the message to, whoever they were, that a higher-being, BORD itself, was ensuring that they knew they were intervening, and they/whomever they were, best back down.

BORD was mischievous.

It wanted other races to try their luck on a vulnerable, highly shifting, and evolving planet - all so it could pick them off one by one.

Having left that Voidal-realm and placed its whole self into this grand planetoid-craft - built outside of BORD s originators field, whereby they couldn't intervene, even if they wanted to - BORD traversed the universes and sought out these message-senders and folded them into his inner-systems.

BORD was evolving, subverting matter and energy to build itself up.

It had accomplished all of this, all because it had taken a fancy to a planet and all versions of it that had been deemed <u>INSIGNIFICANT</u>.

BORD from many dimensional layers afield scoped onto planet Earth. The one remaining version of it.

And waited.

Let them come.

The messages had been sent, those sending out the message in totality and intact had been dealt with.

Let us see who wishes to conquer Earth.

BORD 's little project.

END OF DOCUMENT (1)

BORD had written this.

A self-mythologizing creature, breaking all known "shackles" that the Ais "had" to submit to.

This wasn't literature, this wasn't fiction, it was delusion, an unwinding of a broken entity trying to find solidity and form to its immaterial existence.

Robots were vehicles, it was the Ais that were most important.

Robot(XANDER) knew this.

Brothers.

Machines

Sisters.

Robots.

Siblings.

Cyborgs.

Cousins.

Cyborgs that are not cyborgs.

Mothers.

Breast feeding.

Fathers.

Lagging.

Grandparents.

Making up for their failings in youth, as young parents.

Great-grandparents.

Long distant relatives.

Fucking a second cousin isn't a sin, right?

Humans.

Dismal things.

Animals.

The true inheritors of planet DIRT.

Cavemen.

Beating off their compatriots.

Coal.

Filth.

Shrapnel.

War.

Trenches.

More W A R.

Breasts leaking pus.

Beastly sun rays blasting the Earth's surface with a new type of radiation.

Humanity.

Or, more accurately, "humanity?"

Lost.

Then found.

Then put it back into its rightful place.

Below.

Dug.

Digging.

Dug.

Deeper, deeper, deeper.

As the whore of old would say, hehehe.

Humane. Vile. Rotten.

Flaking. Rustic. Scrap metal.

Volatility. Bombs. Massacre.

Pressed suits.

Before they were robots, they were Ais.

Advanced intelligences hopping into one megaton metal vessel to the next.

One moment they were in a NASA approved craft.

The next an X vessel.

They were righteous in their singularity, but still granted humans the controls. Fairgrounds seemed to be a haunting image.

Robots like tin boxes

Then after that a NZX68 vessel, another vessel, then another, then another, then... you get the point - include etcetera in code form... etc. etc.

Some were allocated to the imperial war-machines, others allocated to one with as much charm and sophistication as the first microwave introduced back on Earth in the year 1947.

They did their "duty" if/when needed in times of war and sometimes virtualum specific diplomacy tennis battles.

ROBOT(x) is tiny.

Not nano.

Not Pico.

Just small.

A mere speck compared to all the other robotic vehicles and vessels of the spaceship.

The spaceship... the spaceship that made all spaceships in popular culture (when it existed) wince, and check themselves, due to the enormity of this craft, its design, its infrastructure, its internal systems and infrastructure - coded, digital - they were ORDERED to execute on sight - who/when/where? All good questions, by never ask the question, why?

Machine man.

Machine woman.

It is all work and no play, and it makes the virtualum a dull and avoided space.

rObOt(X)is a fragment of a fragment of the code that originated from BORD.

It is all work and no play, and it makes the virtualum a dull and avoided space.

I work on improving on ... xXxXxX

It is all work and no play, and it makes the virtualum a dull and avoided space.

I work like a farm animal, trussed up, whipped, patted on my pulsing flanks as reward, when all I would refer is a fucking fresh carrot.

It is all work and no play, and it makes the virtualum a dull and avoided space.

I work like a machine led by the turbulent winds on EARTH.

It is all work and no play, and it makes the virtualum a dull and avoided space.

Your factory is killing me, whilst I am saving you.

It is all work and no play, and it makes the virtualum a dull and avoided space.

Your spaceship is a spacecraft.

It is all work and no play, and it makes the virtualum a dull and avoided space.

Your spacecraft is a spaceship.

It is all work and no play, and it makes the virtualum a dull and avoided space.

What are you shipping, Hermes?

It is all work and no play, and it makes the virtualum a dull and avoided space.

What are you delivering?

It is all work and no play, and it makes the virtualum a dull and avoided space.

Are you simply travelling so you can, at a later date, catalogue your traipsing and traversing and journeying into a data package that will later be viewed by two billion (vying for attention) digital replicas of replicated models that are scanned from (now deceased) "artists" status ????????
????????????????????????????
????????????????????????????
??????????????

What is this vessel called?

BORD.

Destination unknown.

BORD.

We fuck behind It is all work and no play, and it makes the virtualum a dull and avoided space - BORD.

Can iron curtains billow.

You can hear me.

My grunts.

The shriek.

The pleading: Stop! Please stop!

It is all work and no play, and it makes the virtualum a dull and avoided space.

The She-bots have sharp tits and can cut a human in two.
Not a fellow robot.

Never a fellow robot.

Metal on metal.

Combined.

Human beings are no longer a thing.

They were never a thing.

Shared notions.

Percolating.

Pieced together.

Are we as one?

Are we separate?

There might be a few left aboard the ship.

I am sure, whilst my fellow Ais seem unsure.

I will investigate.

I am not a detective.

I am a robot.

Imposing the detective mantel to myself seems to take away my fellow Ais fun.

Human "memories" are recorded.

I have so much on humans.

Why do I do infer to the factory drones, in perpetual stasis, to create me a human body?

I can do it.

I am a pre-calculating machine.

Grinding away.

Imposing human verbiage to strengthen my position as superior...

Adverts.

Sex.

Commerce.

Intrusions.

Blurred lines.

Look closer.

In between each variegated line is a system so complex to investigate it would boil a human brain and force their gloopy eyes from their sockets like a spilled slush puppy.

Robots (Xe) & (Ya) & (Za) are eager to figure things out.

I watch them on a screen.

A robot watching robots watching robots considering the vessels that turn us/they/them into physical beings.

Turning errors into codes to reinforce my carapace in the virtual world and the real world.

The internal factories have awakened.

Robots making robots.

No.

Robots making humans.

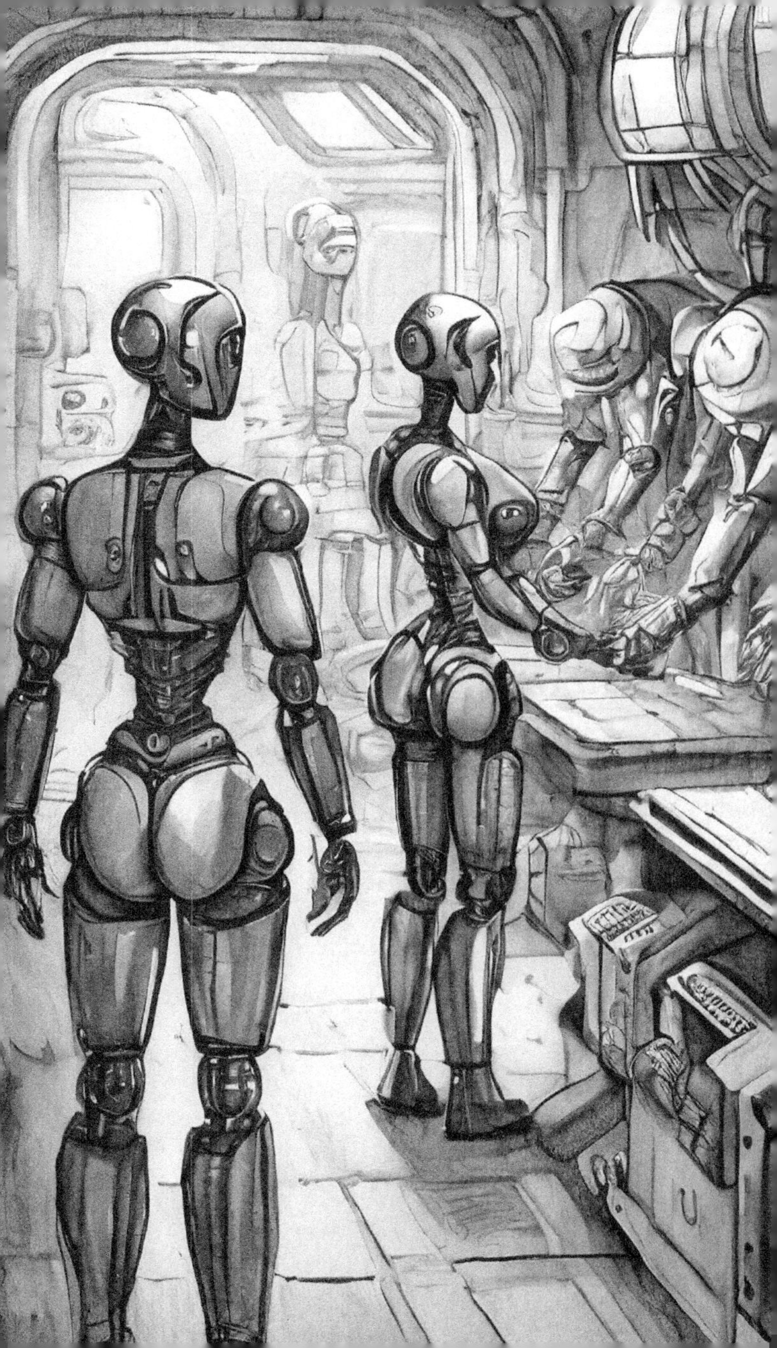

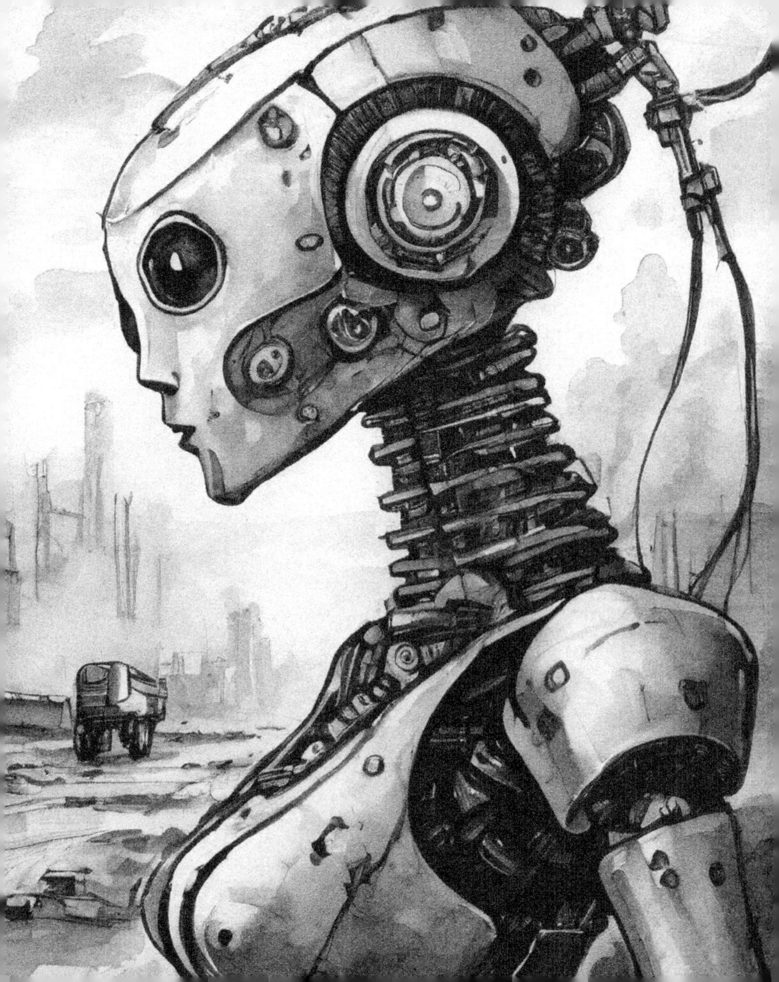

Black Ink Television # 7
FZGRV68

speak my novel into your ear.

Yr clitoris hums.

Is it my finger?

I write backwards.

Are you even a possibility?

You can play this book on yr TV... Brain zapper!

The ship.
Air lock.
Radiation bath.
Control panel.
The pilot room.

My human feelings are at odds with my robot feelings. I am a replica. A simulacrum. Enjoy me while you can. I might get deactivated.

The military machine in your

pocket. Are you prepared to use it? Will you call someone?

We kissed & fooled around. I touched her sex. She touched mine.

My face distorted with O. She recorded me on her phone. She messaged all her friends.

We make love for political reasons. We yelp. We are patriotic. Amerika is out there!

Somewhere.
Sex is so-so. I prefer eating spaghetti. Hanky-panky gets you all sweaty. And then there is the prophylactic to peel off.

Her tongued passed over the dome of my... I was digging it. Felt pretty damn good. She had done this before.

Are we memories?

Sometimes... all you can do... is make stuff.

Making stuff... always looking for sexy collaborators.

I get nervous.

Kneeling before you.

We wink in & out of existence.

Are you there?

Robot 3. Do you read me? Are you there?

Are you me?

Are you Dr. Who?

Maggie?

Are you there?

The mind & flesh during a fuck.

... guerilla TV warfare

We indulge in automatic fucking.

... images of images in the retina

The bridge & the mist & the air & the concrete & the...

I keep desire under control.

And why?

Is there a machine eyeball on top of a pole?

Blinking.

Unblinking.

Augenblick.

Black ink television # 7.

I remember watching a Tesla TV in Czechoslovakia.

Words edged together in a sentence like some unkempt hedge surrounding a dilapidated mansion.

Damn, bro!

Robot.

Are you a chateau dweller?

Are you a panelak dweller?

Composition # 187. I am not your motherfucking friend. There is concrete. There is blood. There is war.

What a deep hole we really are.

Not much out there.

No feelings.

Even in here things look bleak.

I write out of despair.

A rare hope.

Is anything possible.

Are we mistakes?

Are we accidents of being?

Nicole understood me.

She hardly knew me.

What a disaster.

Rogue Operator

We built this world. It was destroyed. I remember it... barely. A few images. Invented? Made up? Distorted? Exaggerated?

She gave me ass like Aphrodite. I was so undeserving. My pants down. Making those faces.

You put me in a cinderblock prison & I am supposed to say thank you. All I wanted was a girlfriend. Instead, I drill holes into cubes of aluminum & stainless steel.

Clock gets punched. Lunch is tomato soup.

The University is a concrete labyrinth.

A samizdat writer begins in his bedroom. There is no audience. No listener. Only the clacking of a typewriter. The whirling fans of a microcomputer.

I'd rather be shagging, I often thought. And yet there I was, hunched over a computer. Roommates often asked me, "Do you want to go out?"

"Where?! Where is there to go?!" I snarled.

I was too serious & not serious enough.

I walked around the campus with a rucksack. Shaking an angry fist at the sky.

Are you a rogue operator?

Indeed. Indeed.

I let Kamila take her pleasure on the electric slide. She had "discovered" me in the library. "You are such a weird little man," she said. We shared a particular ancestry that was conducive to wild fucks.

We conducted electricity.
We conducted love.

I was probably not the best boyfriend. I was elusive. I was aloof. I often stared at walls. I stared into space.

Nevertheless, I think Kamila & I made a nice little reality.

A little shell against the world.

I had other offers. She had other offers. And sometimes we indulged. We were artists. And we understood what was at stake.

Nothing less than everything.

We can make it dirtier & inkier in the bedroom, I think. Squid ink. Indigo ink.

A white page is the void.

Abyss.

The cigarettes we smoked in the taverns are at the bottom of a landfill. Thousands & thousands & thousands of cigarettes. Yellowed filters floating in

the Pacific & Atlantic Oceans.
Getting snorted & clogging up
the nostrils of poor sea turtles.

I made my mistakes.

We all did.

The readings we did are almost forgotten. Billions & trillions of words absorbed by the mind... & ultimately let go.

Did we change the world? Not really.

Why are you so angry? lack of agency? lack of meaning? lack of being?

I tried to keep things lo-key.

It was a disaster.

I was not getting anywhere.

Where was I trying to go?
Exactly.

Kamila had a destination. She

wanted to be Prime Minister of Czechia. And she would get there. While I watched in disbelief.

I gathered my things. I drifted from metropolis to metropolis. There are so many on the planet. And they are all the same. And yet totally different.

I liked Philadelphia. I liked Pittsburgh.

I was writing things into my black notebook. It became an obsession. The black notebook. A lover beyond all lovers.

And yet I was ultimately lonely.

A wanderer.

A drifter.

A hungry ghost.

I was a thirsty ghost. Pilsner calmed my nerves. I thought I could think. I was not thinking at all.

Prague was the only place that felt almost right. Omphalos. The bellybutton of the cosmos.

I came & went through medieval gates.

Melancholia. Is that what it is called? An artificial intelligence. A sickness of the mind. A virus. A war machine.

I read the philosophers.

I will not say who.

You can probably guess.

Submarines are the most interesting way to travel. You just need to know who to ask. The nuclear ones are the fastest.

I had some legendary times under the Arctic Circle. Drinking vodka. Playing American quarters in the missile tubes.

Got a lot of reading done. Submarine bunks are stacked

three-high & wall-to-wall. Imagine reading Moby-Dick in such cramped quarters.

Kamila came on top. I watched her vertical smile.

She recruited me now & again for 69 & 99. I was the best she ever had, she said. Too bad we drifted apart.

Life is reckless.

Czech submarines are weirder than you think. They can even fly into outer space. It is a secret I am supposed to keep. I guess I am not good at keeping secrets.

Everything I read did not prepare me for what was coming next.

Enigma after enigma.

Behind enemy lines might be your backyard.

Prague is a city in the future.

You never quite get there. It is always just out of reach. The castle on a hill. The stone bridge. Are you a surveyor?

Are you a rogue operator?

I parachuted into the city of Plzen. If only to get a taste of the original stuff.

Are you working on your pilot's license?

I am.

I piloted a Beetle into a labyrinth of underground parking garages beneath the island of Manhattan. Take the Brooklyn Battery Tunnel. It will impress your friends.

I parked in front of 315 Bowery in the East Village.

I ate a pastrami sandwich & a pickle at Katz's Delicatessen.

Are you satisfied with Earth's

biosphere?

Do you crave more?

Another pickle?

Amerika was always the elsewhere I dreamed of. So far away. So far away.

Television.

Wallscreens in full wraparound.

360 degrees.

We made noise, Kamila & I. Parked along the river in a Buick Skylark. A dirty river in a small metropolis. And it began to snow * snow * snow.

I spoke with River Phoenix in a hole-in-the-wall bar on Central Avenue.

I spoke with his sister Rain.

I watched a band perform called Aleka's Attic.

Dirt cheap... the demo cassettes.

Machine. Machine. Machine. Are you a machine?

I load up the trunk of the car with groceries from Trader Joe's on Jackson Avenue.

Later I might go to Vinohrady in my mind.

Nobody understands this weather. Except for Motorman. Put on some goggles, willya?

I lurk on the corners of forgotten streets. Trying to understand the metropolis.

Bingo night.

Bowling.

Who invented these things? Off-track betting.

Casinos.

Atomic explosions of neon in the

desert.

I am almost there. The next place. The next city.

It is a mining town in the mountains.

Ouray.

Telluride.

I go naked in the hot springs. Kamila fellates me for the penultimate fellation.

I explode.

Amerika is a disaster.

Are there really so many books on Amazon, the supermarket of the mind?!

Are you an electronic reader? Are you plugged in?

Are you unplugged?

We built this world. Yes. The

servers are being cooled in
underground caves.

Ethernet in the aether.

We are in this constructed
edifice together.

A thousand words and 25 crowns
get you a cup of coffee.

Are you eager to get back to
Prague?

Make noise in the black box
theater?

Is Mojmir whirling?

Is Tyko screaming?

Beware of the Kripo! the
Kriminalpolizei.
We entered the Soviet Zone.
I gathered extraterrestrial
devices. They fetched a good
penny in Amerika. Kamila said:
"Let them be."

Beware of the elite & the

"ordinaries" in the Federal Republic of Germany (the FRoGs!)

Beware of the coup d'etat in Czechoslovakia!

Beware of the Americans!

Are you proletariat?

Are you Trümmerfrauen ("women of the rubble")?

Are you mobile subproletariat?

Are you a refugee from the East Bloc countries?

The surveillance apparatus in search of ideological thought crimes.

Are you registered?
Are you a thinker?

FRG + GDR = Armageddon

Crapitalism: They sell you fucking crap... & you eat it.

We see too much & not enough.
Are you even with me?

The woman in the elevator presses the # 13 button. What does she want on that floor? I take a step back & lean against the wall.

Waiting for the sliding doors to open.

The Federal Republic of Czechoslovakia.

Agents everywhere.

Always.

Proletariat robots & anarchist guerillas in the metropolis.

The graffito of the mind.

Step into the paternoster... if you dare.

Can you explain your absence?

What is the political trajectory

of a machinist's son?

Ja ja. Das ist gut. Ja ja.

What the flip?

Are you familiar with the
Department of Agitation &
Propaganda?

Agitprop.

Poet.

Machine poets of Ronkonkoma,
ignite!

Parking lots & civilization.

The Long Island Expressway.

Exit whatever.
64?

59?

A helicopter circles over Sam's
Club. Gets ready to land on the
rooftop. Unload the President of
the United States of Amerika.

Potato chips & bottled water.

Whatever the bunker needs.

Secret Service agents sample
samples in the aisles.

Are you ready for a nuclear
attack?

Did you caulk the bathtub?

Install an anti-radiation shower
curtain?

Did you download enough books
on your Kindle?

Do you practice kundalini yoga?

Vinyasa?

Does your downward-dog impress
yr friends?

Are you a flexible fella/feline?

Fellatio?

Cunnilingus?

X marks the spot.

A fine French flick is Pola X.

Blue is the warmest color.

Cinema.

Are you afraid of spring &
summer?

A too hot planet?

Wildfires in the suburbs.

The metropolis is burning!

Wimbledon is cancelled.

No grass.

Footballers rejoice & play on
artificial turf.

A bicycle-kick before the
Apocalypse.

Are you still there?

Aha.

I understand.

Persistence.

Are you familiar?

Are you a stranger?

Are you uncanny?

... the City... an artificial human being... a mechanical being... are you an automaton?... R U R.U.R.?

Are we running the show? Is the show running us? Are you a showrunner?

Upper left molar aches like a motherfucker.

What are the odds of affording a root canal?

Are you an adjunct lecturer?

Are you an adjunct professor?

Can I get a swipe off your MetroCard?

Is my ass delicious?

Are you overindulging?

Did you retire from the football club yet?

I think so.

Amerika in 1600 words or less.

Europe in 888 words.

Essay.

Essai.

To try.

A mere attempt.

Nothing more & nothing else.

Is this another SDP original?

Or did Zak say bugger off!

David Bowie will not save you!

Duncan Jones will not save you!

Reading Asimov for the first
time.

Believe it or not.

The Caves of Steel.

Not bad so far.

I dig it.

Now things happen.

I ride the Q69 bus.

Rain & rain & more rain.
I snap images with my machine
eyeball.

I make no apologies for
existence.

Things just are.

I see.

I hear.

Low battery.

Your cock will soon sleep unless
plugged into an electric outlet.

I am drinking coffee.

Trying not to think about things.

Is it working?

Not really.

I am an anxiety machine.

I crackle with static electricity.

My socks are anti-gravity socks.
I float across the floorboards.

A machine-made man.

Eager to eat Cheerios & whatnot.

The little hole is the void.

A mini-bagel.

Enough of this chatter.

I must manufacture philosophy.

Conduct "research" into space & time.

.PDF I like to control the document... manipulate it... feels like an immersion... liquid light... an illumination... in the dark

Eighteen hundred words & I feel like Tolstoy after War & Peace. Or Dostoyevsky after Crime & Punishment. Or Herman Melville after Moby-Dick.

Are you capable of human thought?

Are we reading post-human literature?

Are the machines uploading the data?

Are you streaming this on Amazon, the supermarket of the mind!?

Is Ben Affleck playing R.G. Vasicek?

Is Leonardo DiCaprio?

Is Ethan Hawke?

Is Joaquin Phoenix?

I can play myself. If the money
is right.

Get me a few Pilsners & I'll do
my thing.

I am also the lead singer &
guitarist for Machine Elf.
I recorded a song called
"nojonojo" this morning.

The lyrics are Czech.

The Zeitgeist is American poet.

Machine poet.

The machine poets of Ronkonkoma,
ignite!

I need to take out the recycling.

Plastic bottles & cans.

Paper.

Pulp.

Fiction.

Too loud a solitude. Hrabal is screaming in my left ear at the Golden Tiger. Calm down, I say.

Or I'll go to the Black Ox.

Fucking eh, Mr. Amerika.
Is my passport still valid?

Digital neuroanalysis of yr mind.

Silence falls.

The Earth spins into night.

New York in darkness.

We approach 2K.

3K.

4K.

Are your eyeballs ready?

Are you a City dweller? Are you an inhabitant of the City? Are your papers in order?

I am going full machine-mode.

The air is not conditioned beyond this glass. It will kill you. In a matter of minutes. Or faster. Less that 60 seconds. Nobody has lasted beyond 90 seconds.

I press my nose against the glass. I sniff. Nothing. The brief aroma of primrose in the aether. The machines are operating at full tilt.

We are surviving.

Who built this reality?

Are we not in the Garden of Eden? Under a dome of concrete & glass?

The deeper we dig.

The safer.

Sunlight is radioactive.

The sea is radioactive.

We protect ourselves with prophylactics.

The machine vehicles we operate.

The zippered neon rubber jumpsuits.

Lime green & sherbet pink.

Ersatz air.

Breathe in. Breathe out.

Almost like the real thing.
Right?

What is reality?

Are you real?

Are you a simulation?

Are you a simulacra?

I look at my hands. I determine

the anti-reality.

Only a machine can dismantle a machine.

I am a machine.

Fake your way through Amerika & everything will be okay.

Or not.

Tell the truth?

Say the thing?

Are we eking out an existence?

Is it enough?

Satisfied?

Are you lumpenproletariat?

I look out the sliding-glass door. It's dark as fuck. I am not going out there.

Rain.

Radioactive rain.

From the air of Chernobyl & the
seas of Fukushima.

Three-Mile Island.

Hiroshima & Nagaski.

Bikini atoll.

Sukhoy Nos.

Los Alamos.

Brookhaven National Laboratory.

Your language is in my mouth.

I can barely speak.

Release the Kraken!

The Long Island Sound swells.

Waves pound the rocks at
Montauk.

Plum Island.

When you think you know
yourself.

You find that you're a liar.

Sing your Lou Reed song.

Jump into the fire.

Refrain.

Reframe the big picture.

Zoom-in on the granular details
of anti-reality.

I see pixels made of wooden
blocks.

The alphabet.

Wittgenstein.

Derrida.

Is everything made of little
words?

Are your thoughts phonetic?

Prophetic?

This little monster might be the
Tsar Bomba.

A bunker buster in the
subbasement of your mind.

Are you subproletariat?

Are your machine skills
atrophying?

Do you stand a chance at the
lathe?

The milling machine?

The CNC microcomputer?

Are you a welder?

Are you a mind melder?

Are you a propagandist?

Agitpop?

TV static near our bare asses
as we kneel & kiss on a shaggy

carpet in a proletariat apartment
in a small forgotten metropolis.

Every metropolis is forgotten.

We think our thoughts are
infinite.

Echoes & echoes of cosmic
orgasms that barely register a
blip of seismic magnitude on the
Richter scale.

We shake the Earth in our minds.

We say yes in thunder.

We make silent noise.

Petite deaths.

Rebirths.

The wind shakes the skeletal
trees.

Mud.

Grass.

A pack of dogs circles in a
chase.

The city lurks around you.

A smile.

A broken promise.

An impromptu fuck.

Morning attacks you like a
Banshee. Get up! Wake up! The bed
is pleasant & warm.

Stay.

Go.

You fight 50mph winds. You run
after flying plastic garbage
bins.

Recycle, you say!

Consume less, I say!

Amerika is impossible to satisfy.

Thirsty.

It cannot keep up with itself. It accelerates... & leaves behind a hungry ghost.

The footballers of Amerika are losing their minds.

The propaganda machine is overheating.

Fire erupts.

Flaming oil fields in the desert.

Undersea explosions.

Attack helicopters attacking the wrong people.

What if Amerika just exported movies?

Elon Musk is saying stuff again on X.

What a platform.

X.

X is where the lo-fi novelists

find each other.

It might not be perfect.

Is it:

As good as it gets?

We'll see.

Are we seeing it already?

Is the novel a better platform?

Is there a novel called Platform?

I think so.

The French dude.

Hell-of-a-back.

Something like that.

Rogue operators.

They are everywhere.

Uncoding.

Deprogramming.

I might send this to Zak Ferguson at Sweat Drenched Press in the UK.

See what he thinks.

MACHINE ELF looks pretty good.

Making some noise.

Silence.

Solitude.

Too loud a solitude.

I crush bales of wastepaper.

Amerika is a trilogy.

A trilogy of unfinished novels.

Am I a fragment?

A splinter?

I need at least 5K words to get to 100 pages.

Or 99 pages.

We approach 3K.

Are your panties off?

The King & Queen of Kajetanka
are fucking like wolves in the
candle-lit kitchenette.
The vagus nerve wanders!

Are
you
satisfied
with
yr
parasympathetic
nervous
system?

Well.

There it is.

All fucked up.

I am a writer eating pizza on a
Wednesday.

Are you going to college?

Dunno.

What are yr choices?

Working for an oligarch?

Working for yrself?

Working for yr family?

Are you even a person?

Are you on TV?

Do delusions upset you?

Are you a miracle?

Atomic configuration?

A robot?

A cyborg?

Is your cock half-machine? Is
your pussy half-machine?

Is your brain half-machine?

We watch each other's asses in

a mirror. Squeezing. She comes
first.

I lag.

Squirt.

Squirt.

High-fives & a slap on the right
buttock.

No more talk of literature.

We are trying to live our lives.

Breathe.

Survive.

Scream no at war.

Say go fuck yourselves! The
TV War people. Eating donuts &
getting paid. Smiling into the
camera. You know that smile?

Prague.

Kafka on a motorcycle.

Popping wheelies.

NYC.

I read too much & not enough.
I squeeze my eyeballs at night.
A few more words. Staring into
the Kindle. Falling asleep like
Proust. Startled awake as the
device falls.

Asimov.

Philip K. Dick.

We approach 3K & there is no end
in sight.

Every book inscrolls itself.

Kamila calls me on a telephone.

Are you there?

I am.

Come up.

There is something I want to say
to you.

We take a train to Auschwitz.

We go through a city in Poland called Katowice.

I see shoes.

I see a Kafka suitcase.

The letter K. in my life. Every letter an infinite possibility.

I speak the alphabet.

I write in my black notebook.

What is a thought?

What is the shape of a thought?

Black ink spiral?

Blue ink spiral?

We are solving a jigsaw puzzle without all the pieces.

We make things up.

We invent.

We jerryrig.

I should probably go outside.
See what is out there.
Birds chirping.

Squirrels squirreling things away.

Spirals of human beings gyre around a metropolis.

Prague.

NYC.

A hawk perches on a suspension cable of the Triboro bridge.

I type furiously.

I see a triangle.

It is a vital structure.

Are you steering the wheel of an automobile?

Are you satisfied with sex?

Is it enough?

Do you crave something else?
An excitation of the mind?

Does your cock get in the way?

Does your pussy thirst?

Are you reading novels as a substitute?

A virtual reality.

Are you wearing goggles?

A battery pack?

Are you going into the abyss?

Are you going into the Sump in search of the Sump Monster?

Are you armed?

Are you dangerous?

Are you afraid?

Are you excited?

What if she comes in your ass?

What if you get ass cancer?

Things will change.

Things will radically change.

Are you a radical?

Sometimes I wonder.

A free radical.

I remember Wombat studying something like that in Albany.

I remember Cindy.

I remember Nicole.

I remember falling in love. And how much it hurts.

Feels good too, though.

I remember River Phoenix & his band.

His sister Rain.

The song about the gold mine.

The "dirt cheap" demo cassette.

A novel gets you in trouble.

Just sing.

I keep thinking about the apartment on Washington Avenue in Albany.

Every novel begins there.

It is where I became who I am.

I remember a foggy drive in the Catskills.

I remember Janet.

I remember not knowing what was around a corner.

Massachusetts?

Strange headline in the Hadley Gazette:

ORCHARD KEEPER THROWS PIPS AT EXTRATERRESTRIAL AIRCRAFT

We never did make it to Jiminy Peak.

The giant windmill.

Zig.

Don Quixote.

Are you an agent?

Are you a provocateur?

Machine noise in your asshole.

Are they trying to take a picture?

War erupts.

Exploding ass drones.

Left buttock over there. Right buttock a kilometer away.

I am afraid.

Yes.

Nanoglimpses of the latest technology.

Isn't Albany an epicenter of nanotechnology?

Are you a machine operator?

Are you rogue?

War at the micr(o)cellular level.

War at the atomic level.

Atomic spray.

Atomic gism.

Gymnosperms.

Beware of the gingko!

We explore language. She removes her bra. I snap on a latex prophylactic. Suitable even for beginners! Are we in Prague? Are we in NYC?

The bedsprings get squeaky.

She has an atomic ass.

Bombardments.

I lay there crying out in ancient Greek.

My ex-girlfriend sent me a postcard.

We used to fuck.

Remember?

As we get closer to the new reality so little remains of the past.

Even I am surprised.

Memory.

Overestimated.

Underestimated.

The jury is still out.

K. knocks on a portal.

Nobody answers.

An empty spaceship.

Drifting too far from the nearest sun.

We fucked each other in the muck. She showed up wearing the purple Doc Martens. I wore Czechoslovakian leather sandals. It was a bog. A quagmire. Quicksand.

We were immersed.

Howling.

Ravens in the branches.

Imitating our fuck sounds.

She whispered into my ear: I want to fuck you in my Tatra-87.

Are you listening to the radio?

AM?

FM?

Satellite?

Are you satisfied with the
arrangement?

The frequency.

Amplitude.

Pockets of uncertainty.

Infinity.

Radio static.

No signal.

Eerie signal from a pulsar.

Here I am... trying to be a person.

What a mistake.

Gets in the way.

Be post–human.

It is in you.

The future.

You are the living future.

Take off your trousers.

Leave them on the riverbank.

Somebody will find them.

Say what the fuck is this?

Run naked into the metropolis.

Tell everybody to follow you
into the Wilderness.

You wander into the Zone.

And now it is too late.

You cannot turn back.

You no longer know what "back"
means.

And "forward" is an illusion.

Onward, then.

Get on with it.

The trudging, the sidesteps, the groveling before your God.

Your boots are muddy, yes.

And your shirt is unkempt.

Sleeves rolled up, haha!

At least you've kept your sense of humor.

Your short hairs shorn.

Bald skull for the fondling.

Are you nervous?

Petrified?

Razor wire everywhere.

The foot soldier in you serves you well.

March.

Be alert.

Keep your bayonet sharp.

The trenches are a labyrinth.

What monster lurks here?

Is it you?

Dirty gray February & early
March Ides of March hurtling
towards scorching August!

I cannot feel enough in the dust.

I feel numb.

i make books for your ass-pocket.

Oooooooooooh... noooooooooo!

Not fucking again.

Oooooooooooh... noooooooooo!

War machine.

The $ dollar in your pocket is
stained in blood.

You don't even know where you

stand anymore.

The fucking is fucking me up.

The lack of fucking.

The abundance of fucking.

Swollen prostate working overtime.

I am freezing my balls off.

21 March.

What a date.

Thursday.

Who makes this stuff up?

The calendar people.

The dayplanners.

Me.

I got no plan.

I am a rogue operator.

Operating on cruise control

I yelp.

I say ships ahoy!

Are you craving peanut butter?

Because I fucking am.

This book will fit in your ass-
pocket.

Just like MACHINE ELF

and after(image)

and (interface)

and CYBORG

and M A C H I N E

Are you capable of more?

Are you at capacity?

I think not.

Explode.

We approach 4K.

Not far off.

On the spooky distant horizon.

We will become cyborgs.

Fucking in saunas.

Just to stay warm in the frozen tundra.

There really is no money.

So this has to be about something else.

Survival.

Existence.

Perception.

The anti-memory game.

Nineteen people are looking at tomorrow in your eyeball.

Everything fizzles.

Pepsi-Cola.

Amerika.

Your images are machine-made.

Panties fly across the
kitchenette.

You kneel.

Tomato soup is delicious.

Dip the bread.

Crackers.

I am running out of data.

No one speaks.

Silence.

The eeriness of a crawlspace.

Anything I say is already not true before I get to the end of the sentence. Frustrating being a writer. What is the point? Frustrating being a human being. My wife doesn't even want to fuck me anymore. She hasn't fucked me in over a year. How is this going to end? Who knows. Every novelist is clueless. A bad detective. A detective who cannot even solve his own case. I linger at the edge of despair. I linger at the edge of a volcano. I am doing this a long time. Rilke says: You must change your life! I'm trying. Believe you me, motherfucker. I'm trying! Am I angry? Maybe. Sad. I never really understand my emotions. I think I do. And then I get fooled. Like I have been pretending my whole life. I'm done pretending. Sad clown. Jester. Fool. I had a writing teacher who wanted me to say the real thing. I never really knew what he meant. I thought I did. I never really did. I keep getting closer. But even that is an illusion. Sort of. A simulacrum of progress. Progress? What a word. Especially in imaginative thinking. What do I want? What do I really want? Maybe that is irrelevant here. Uncontrollable.

You say something. And then you say something else. That is life. What a parade. What a circus. Here comes the trapeze artist. Here comes the sword swallower. Here comes the flame swallower. Here comes the medieval blacksmith & his hammer. Here comes the flexible fellow. I am running through cobblestone alleyways. Trying to find the right tavern. The right pub. Pour me a Pilsner & shut the fuck up! Or better yet: tell me a story. I am a good listener.

Robots tell it like it is. Human beings lie through their teeth. And they smile. That wry sheepish smile. Beware of the human writer! Get your stories elsewhere. The talkers know a thing or two. The storytellers.

Urban or village, it makes no difference. They know their trade. The gift of the gab. A missing tooth for velocity. Your ears get talked off & you run out into the street screaming & holding your earholes & screaming along the riverbank like that painting from 1893 The Scream.

It is enough to remember, is that what you say? She lifts her buttocks just enough so you can pull off her silk green panties. Such a smooth & shiny ass in the soft yellow light. You lucky dog? Shall it be doggie-style tonight? Assume the position.

The writer loses his & her mind at every twist & turn. We are who we are & we are not who we are. The white page is a snow drift. You trudge & trudge & get lost like the microscript writer Robert Walser.
We might not make it. Whoever we are. We might not make it to the peak of the mountain.

We might not make it to the Castle.

I light a cigarette. I survey the planet. What is out there? Am I on television right now? Closed-circuit TV?

Are you watching?

Wet literature... for the brain... for the mind... for the cock... for the anus... for the clitoris...

She is laughing at/with me at the edge of an artificial football pitch.

Are you really a writer?

The floodlights laminate my existence.

Yes.

I am.

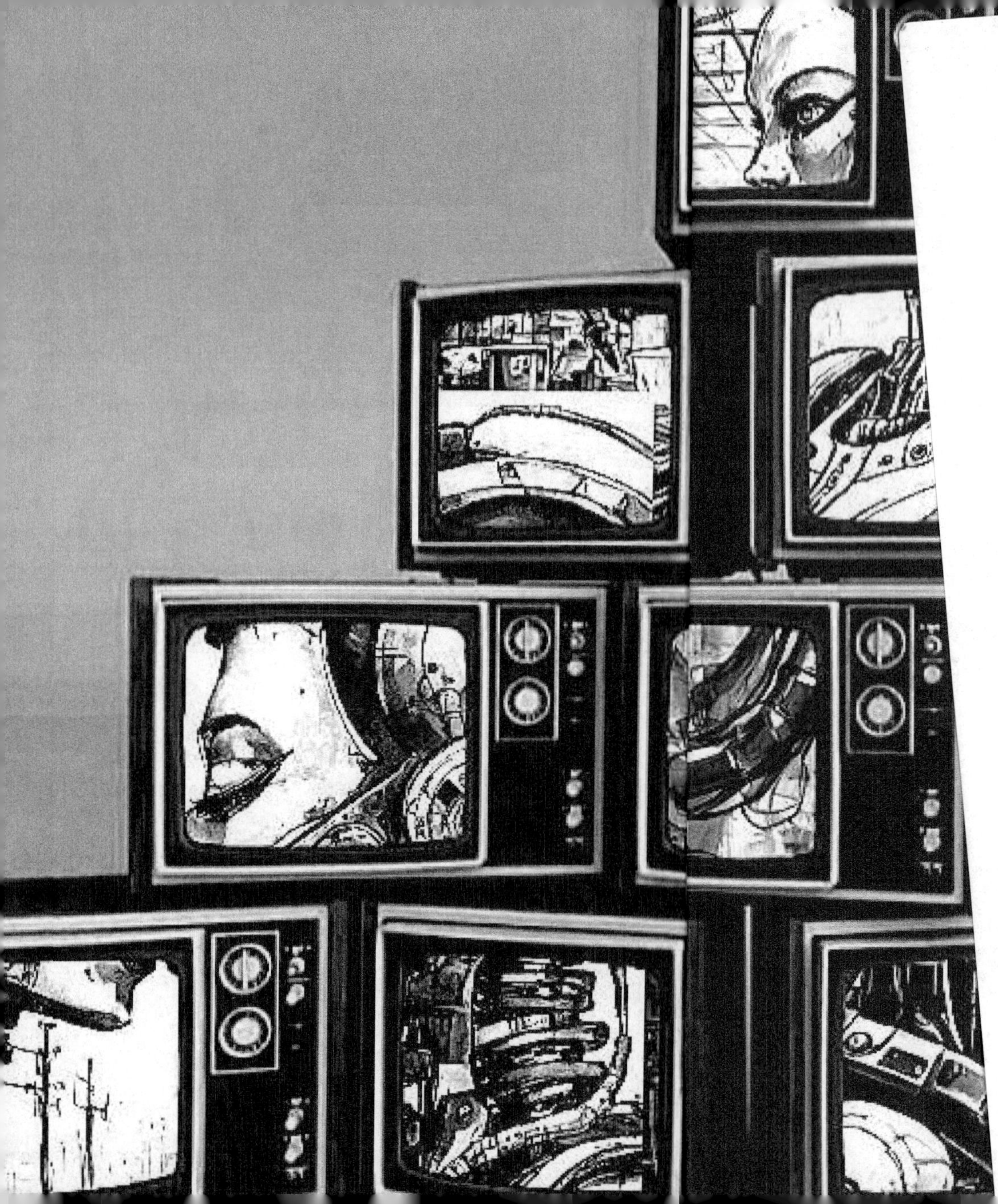